# ONTARIO
## *Garlic*

### THE STORY FROM FARM TO FESTIVAL

PETER McCLUSKY

THE
History
PRESS

Published by The History Press
Charleston, SC 29403
www.historypress.net

*Cover images*: Front cover: Metechi garlic, Marbled Purple Stripe variety. *Photo by Peter McClusky*; Garlic farmer Bob Baloch in bottom left. *Courtesy of Bob Baloch*; Ontario garlic in bottom middle. *Courtesy of Peter McClusky*; Courtney Dutchak at the Wychwood winter farmers' market in bottom right. *Photo by Peter McClusky*. Back cover: Garlic field ready for planting, Golden Acres Farm, Gads Hill, Ontario; life portrait of Ted Maczka, the "Garlic Man," by Igor Babailov, Hon. RAA.

First published 2015

Manufactured in the United States

ISBN 978.1.62619.920.0

Library of Congress Control Number: 2015936861

*Notice*: The information in this book is true and complete to the best of our knowledge. It is offered without guarantee on the part of the author or The History Press. The author and The History Press disclaim all liability in connection with the use of this book.

To my brothers and sisters,
and to my wife, Deborah.

# CONTENTS

# Hardneck Garlic Plant

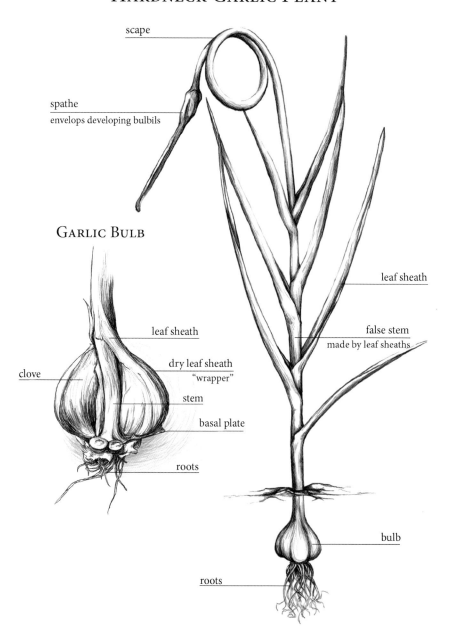

scape

spathe
envelops developing bulbils

## Garlic Bulb

leaf sheath

clove

dry leaf sheath
"wrapper"

stem

basal plate

roots

leaf sheath

false stem
made by leaf sheaths

bulb

roots

Mature hardneck garlic plant and bulb (*Allium sativum var. ophioscorodon*). *Courtesy of Toronto Garlic Festival.*

*Preface*

# THE ACCIDENTAL FARMER

*Looking for a crop to plant in the fall, I was told, "tulips or garlic."*

Until the spring of 2009, I lived and breathed stock photos. I headed international distribution for a New York digital stock photo company. The CEO left me to my own devices to bring in new business. I traveled to more than thirty countries, visiting places like Kiev, Budapest, Hong Kong, Sydney, Buenos Aires, Vancouver, Lisbon and Paris. I loved the challenges and the people. I even loved sitting in airport lounges. Back at the headquarters in Midtown Manhattan, I kept plants in the window. I figured whenever we did an office shuffle, the office manager would take pity on me and my plants. Sure enough, not only did I survive multiple layoffs and buyouts, but I also always managed to have a desk beside a window. Thank you, philodendrons, weeping fig and Boston fern.

After eleven years, I started to question what I was doing. I couldn't articulate it at the time, but I knew there had to be something more. Could I afford such a change financially? No. Could my mental well-being endure at this job? No. Something had to give. I had a vague inkling of something connected to farming, but I had no idea how or why. I said goodbye to Manhattan and returned to my hometown, Toronto. My sister suggested that I volunteer with one of the small-plot farmers at FarmStart in Brampton. In return for helping plant and weed her vegetables, farmer Kate Hamilton gave me a small patch to grow my own vegetables. I soon learned that farming a small plot of land is a different beast than what I was used to. It wasn't as simple as calling from an airport boarding gate to the office to ask a colleague to water my philodendron. And garlic? It was something I cooked with. It had no special place in my life.

My utter ignorance of all things botanical came to the fore by the end of the season at FarmStart. My little patch in Kate's quarter-acre plot had failed. My heirloom tomatoes were as dry as rusted barbed wire. Squash vines were strangled by vicious weeds like sea serpents entwined in a battle to the death. My celery was as thin and limp as overcooked vermicelli. I could hardly call it a vegetable patch—it was more like a lunar landscape. On my last visit, I did discover a single squash. It was green, shiny and the size of a bowling ball. Using my pocketknife, I gingerly cut it loose from the gnarled wreckage of weeds and withered vines. I walked across the field to my car, holding it close to my chest like it was a Fabergé egg. I all but fastened a seatbelt around that squash for the end-of-season ride home. Hundreds of car trips to my plot in Brampton and back again and just one squash to show for it. That ten-pounder must have had a carbon footprint the size of a Tyrannosaurus.

That night, as my wife and I slurped squash soup, I resolved not to end the season on a sour note. I wanted to plant something I could harvest in the spring. The next morning, I called around to some farmers. I learned that there are two common crops planted in the fall in Canada: tulips and garlic. One farmer in particular, Robert Litke, said that he'd send me "a few bulbs of garlic."

I later learned that Bob was a philosophy professor at Wilfrid Laurier University. He was holed up, at the time, in his farmhouse in Gadshill, Ontario, researching and writing about Friedrich Nietzsche. I guess he was stuck on a particularly tricky aspect of Nietzsche because a month after my call I'd still not received the promised garlic. I was about to start making phone calls—about tulips—when a large box arrived in the mail. Inside were several brown paper bags. Sitting at my desk with the box perched on my lap, I reached inside and randomly grabbed a bag. Like a jeweler emptying rare gems from a velvet pouch, I let the contents tumble onto the desk. I'd never seen or imagined garlic like this. I picked up a bulb and held it to the light. The wrappers clung tightly to the bulb and were translucent, like porcelain, and streaked with hues of red and purple. I pulled more bags from the box, careful not to mix the contents. Bob had scribbled strange-sounding names on each bag: Yampolski and Choparsky, Russian Red, Siberian Red, Hungarian, Georgian Fire and Czech Broadleaf. Two hundred bulbs in all, enough for one thousand

Bob Litke inspects a garlic bulb at Golden Acres Farm in Gads Hill, Ontario. *Photo by Peter McClusky.*

cloves. I pictured endless garlic stalks waving in the breeze. My next challenge? Where to plant them.

During my year at FarmStart, I had met Bob Baloch, a farmer and IT consultant. (He later became a garlic vendor at the Toronto Garlic Festival.) Bob generously offered me some space on his plot to plant my garlic. Once my one thousand garlic cloves lay snuggled under a thick straw mulch, I breathed a sigh of relief. But there was more to learn. How was I going to harvest the garlic? Where would I store it? I didn't want to repeat my mistakes that had led to the single squash. Daniel Hoffman, another farmer I cold-called and later got to know, introduced me to the idea of farm internships.

*Left*: Ontario Hardneck garlic bulbs come in many sizes. *Photo by Peter McClusky.*

*Below*: Artichoke variety, Transylvanian strain, is a softneck garlic grown at Golden Acres Farm. *Photo by Peter McClusky.*

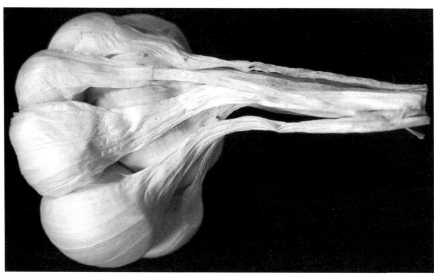

Ontario farmer Daniel Hoffman offers several strains of his heirloom garlic at the Toronto Garlic Festival. *Photo by Peter McClusky.*

After a bit more research I came across an ad from a farm near Guelph, Ontario:

> *Whole Circle Farm offers an eight month farm internship…spring begins with tapping for maple syrup and work on the garden starts in the greenhouse, followed by raising of livestock, working the field, selling produce, making compost and biodynamic preps, food preservation, building and tractor maintenance; plus field trips and in-field and in class education. Weekly stipend comes with room and board and access to vehicles. Twelve hour days start at 6 am.*

"Twelve-hour days?" Who would commit to something like that? I snickered smugly as I read the ad to my wife…but she didn't laugh. Turns out that she knew me better than I knew myself. Four weeks later, I started an eight-month internship at Whole Circle Farm near Acton, Ontario.

The other interns were half my age, and the weekly stipend was what I'd regularly spent on a lunch at a restaurant two doors from my New York office on West 18th Street. Almost twenty years in New York had hardwired

Farm steward Johann Kleinsasser inspects the soil at Whole Circle Farm, near Acton, Ontario. *Photo by Peter McClusky.*

my brain to a different sort of life. My mind was still not in this new world. So, on my second day on the farm, when I sleepily clutched a cow's teat during the 6:00 am milking, my face scrunched against her warm flank, I half-thought I was holding the safety bar on the N/R express train to Manhattan. For the first month, I kept my packed suitcases under my bed with the handles facing out.

Eventually, I settled into the routine at Whole Circle Farm. They taught me a lot about farming, growing garlic and especially about land stewardship and soil. It's all about the soil. The metre of topsoil that covers most of the earth's surface is crucial to our survival—it's where our food comes from—and is little understood.

In the second year of garlic growing, I planted ten thousand cloves—this time on a quarter-acre patch I rented from Whole Circle Farm. While thinking of avenues to sell all that garlic, I got the idea of starting the Toronto Garlic Festival. Why not bring a festival to the city?

In my third year of growing garlic, I planted twenty-five thousand cloves. Like a desk-bound general reviewing battle plans, it all looked good on paper, but it turned out to be a bridge too far. I had been intoxicated by the mysterious names and ended up planting forty-five different strains of garlic. Planting was the easy part. The following summer, the weeding and harvest nearly killed me. After one particularly long day in the field, I lay in bed clutching a bottle of painkillers, with a hot water bottle pressed desperately against my back.

Before I dozed off, my mind started to wander. I pictured the rows and rows of garlic I'd hand-harvested disappearing off into the distance. If all my beds of garlic were laid end to end, would they equal two and a half CN Towers? Those hazy calculations swirled around and around until they were permanently lodged in my head. Now, whenever I look up at the CN Tower, I'm taken back to those days on the farm—back to when I used my four-door city car like a pickup truck, transporting freshly harvested garlic from the field to the barn, half a mile away, with bundled garlic stalks protruding from every window. My crazy days as a garlic power broker are behind me. Now I grow a more manageable five to ten thousand plants from about eight different strains. I can hand-plant about six-hundred cloves in an hour, and with the staggered maturation period of each strain, harvesting is manageable.

After all those years in New York City, did I make the right decision? Was I destined to become a farmer? There was no epiphany; that only happens in movies. It was the little decisions that led to this—that and my small triumphs. Farming helped me overcome my insecurities and ignore my fears.

But what if I had stayed in New York? Would I still be selling photos of garlic instead of growing it? Maybe. However, the company I worked for was sold, and everyone was let go. Perhaps there was something in the soil, calling me back to Ontario. And I'm glad I listened to it.

# ACKNOWLEDGEMENTS

My aunt Nina has been gardening for eighty-two years. The last few years she made room for some garlic plants. When she did that, I knew I was on to something good.

To write this book, I interviewed more than 150 people and enjoyed hearing their personal garlic stories. At times, I felt like the Alfred Kinsey of garlic: "When was your first garlic experience?" "Who introduced you to it?" "Was the sensation hot?…Spicy?" "Did you hide your enjoyment (of garlic) from others?" People were extremely supportive in their responses. I could only include a few of their stories in my book, but together their diverse perspectives provided me the grounding I needed.

There are many more people I wish I'd had the chance to interview. While some nationalities and groups were not specifically mentioned, I hope this book captures the essence of the universal story of garlic.

Ontario's garlic—and this book—would be nothing without Ontario farmers and farming advocates. Many thanks to Sri Sethuratnum, Bob Litke, Daniel Hoffman, Bob Baloch, Paul Pospisil and Kate Hamilton. They gave me a leg up, and a few bulbs of garlic, when I was just starting out. Johann and Maggie Kleinsasser at Whole Circle Farm, together with farm manager Abe Wahi, graciously accepted me as an intern on their farm for eight months in 2010—it was an awakening.

Thanks to Professor Rina Kamenetsky Goldstein, Institute of Plant Sciences, Agricultural Research Organization, the Volcani Center, Israel, for input on the morphology of *Allium sativum*. I thank the following for advice on the chapter about growing garlic: Bart Brusse (Sheridan Nurseries); Colette Murphy (Urban Harvest); Tarrah Young (Being Green Farm); and Julie Fleishauer (Golden Acres Farm). Also, Becky Hughes, head, Northern Horticultural Research/SPUD Unit, New Liskeard Agricultural Research Station, University of Guelph, and Michael Celetti, plant pathologist, Horticulture Crops Program Lead at Ontario Ministry of Agriculture, Food and Rural Affairs, University of Guelph, for valuable input on plant disease and pests. And thanks to Bridget Wranich, Fort York National Historic Site, for input on garlic's historic context.

Thanks to Professor Eric Block, Department of Chemistry, University of Albany, for help in deciphering the chemistry of *Allium sativum*. Dr. Block has been at the forefront of research into the chemistry of garlic for more than forty years and has given a talk on garlic chemistry at the Toronto Garlic Festival.

Thanks to Serge Avery for his comments on ancient central Asia. Thanks to Ane Christensen and my brother, John, and sister, Cathy, for their creative feedback.

Elizabeth Driver's landmark bibliographic work, *Culinary Landmarks*, was an immense help in researching Canadian and Ontario cookbook history. Thanks also to members of the Culinary Historians of Canada. Thanks to Julia Rickert at the Institute of Holistic Nutrition and interns from the institute: Brigitte Fiorino, Jacquie Thompson, Liane Beam-Wansbrough and Maggie Millwood. Thanks also to researchers Mimi McDowell and Aaron Kniznik.

The following archives, libraries and institutions provided valuable archival information: City of Greater Sudbury Archives; Exhibition Place—Records and Archives, Toronto; Schlesinger Library, Radcliffe Institute, Harvard University; Thomas Fisher Rare Book Library; and the Marilyn & Charles Baillie Special Collections Centre at Toronto Public Library.

Thank you to Mary and John Stefura and members of the Ukrainian Seniors Centre, Sudbury; and Sonia Aimy Oduwa for assistance with chef introductions.

Daniel Garber, my editor and writing coach, provided an objective perspective and a voice of clarity in the editing and shaping of this book from its first proposal until the final version. Thanks to Ryan Finn and Marje Dixon for the final edits.

My wife, Deborah, is extraordinarily creative, imaginative, inspiring and supportive. I couldn't imagine this journey without her.

Aside from archival research, the heart of this book comes from the stories—and, in some cases, recipes—told by the following individuals:

# ACKNOWLEDGEMENTS

Julia Aitken, Steve Anderson, Daniel Ansu, Seymore Applebaum, John Arena, Mario Aricci, Dominic Badali, Sal Badali, Jennifer Bain, Bob Baloch, Bruce Bell, Rodney Bowers, Halia Buba, Mike Buba, Ed Burt, Massimo Capra, Patrick Carter, James Chatto, Ane Christensen, George Cleary, David Colhmeyer, Wayne Conway, Arnold Cornelius, Greg Couillard, Alan Cowan, Pat Crocker, Mark Cullen, Chef D, Sonia Day, Simon de Boer, Rita DeMontis, Ivonete de Sousa, Argentino del Piero, Arlene del Piero, Christina Dixon, Donna Dooher, Peter Dyer, Kirk Elliott, Josie Emond, Kaniz Fatima, Alexandra Feswick, Joe Fiorito, Kathy Flint, Jenny Forte, Roberto Fracchioni, Kevin Frank, Lynn Freeman, Alison Freyer, Eileen Garber, Brad Goulding, Barry Gragg, Wayne Greer, Rob Gregorini, Donna Griffith, Jean Gural, JP Gural, Warren Ham, Kate Hamilton, Lloyd J. Harris, John Higgins, Daniel Hoffman, Curt Hospidales, Jason Huang, Chung-Ja Jackson, Stan Jeong, Mel Jones, Josh Josephson, Jamie Kennedy, Graham Kerr, Michael Kidus, Banchi Kinde, Tom Kioussis, Marie Klassen, Johann Kleinsasser, Dinah Koo, Dorothy Lane, Lorraine Lazarenko, Jason Lee, Soyoung Lee, Mrs. Lee, Susur Lee, Theresa Lemieux, Emily Leonard, Marilyn Lightstone, Chris Likourgiotis, Karon Liu, Brad Long, Shirley Lum, Nina MacDonald, Heather MacMillan, Ted Maczka, Bryan Mailey, Tiferanji Malithano, Sanjiz Mathews, Célestin Mbanianga, Cathy McClusky, Joanne McClusky, John McClusky, Mike McClusky, Susan McClusky, Chris McDonald, John McDougall, Gretchen McDowell, Mark McDowell, Bruce McEwen, Anna McGrenaghan, Alex McKay, Stuart McLean, Mary Luz Mejia, Ennio Mercantonio, Rod Meyers, Peter Minaki, Corey Mintz, Jordan Mitchell, Mark Mitchell, Peter Mitchell, Scott Mitchell, Aisha Mohamed, Helena Moroz, Amy Morris, Wayne Morris, Mike Murakami, Colette Murphy, Al Music, Sivakumar Nadarajah, Subagini Nadarajah, Bart Nagel, Zarqa Nawaz, Brenda Norman, Vanesha Nuckchaddee-Khadaroo, Laurie Oehy, Marilyn Onucky-Vervega, Giacomo Pasquini, Aman Patel, Edo Pehilj, Joan Pond, Paul Pospisil, Ron Raymer, Sheila Robb, Bob Romaniuk, Irene Romaniuk, Cookie Roscoe, Harry Rosen, Suman Roy, Tony Sabherwal, Jessica Schmidt, Len Senator, Sridharan Sethuratnam, Sandra Sharko, Roma Shewciw, Mandeep Singh, Matthew Smerek, Anne Sorrenti, Michael Stadtländer, John Stefura, Mary Stefura, Mike Strathdee, Richard Szpin, Peter Tsaras, Stella Walker, Anne Waters, Adam Waxman, Sara Waxman, Jacqui Wice, Mary Williamson, Ted Woloshyn, Evelyn Wu, Anne Yarymowich and Monika Zhu.

# GARLIC COMES KNOCKING

*Mum would have nothing to do with the garlic seller,*
*and I always stayed away from him, too.*

—*Kirk Elliott*

The Hamilton police didn't consider it a breaking and entering. The Elliotts had left the doors and windows of their red brick house wide open that unseasonably warm fall day in 1959. "That was the day Mum surprised an intruder in her kitchen." Kirk Elliot told me the story of his family's first encounter with garlic.

Clifford Elliott, Kirk's father, was a well-respected United Church minister and radio announcer in Hamilton, Ontario. His wife, Patricia, was a Juilliard-trained musician, originally from a small town in Saskatchewan. They lived with their three kids—Cherry, twelve; Kirk, eight; and Stuart, four—on Holton Avenue. In that neighbourhood, you could still see the milkman in a horse-drawn wagon and an iceman who delivered the cold blocks by hand:

> *Mum was not a typical minister's wife. Cooking a turkey meant putting it in the oven for a very long time, maybe with some stuffing inside. That afternoon, she was roasting the turkey to death. Mum and Dad were relaxing out back when I saw a man in the kitchen. He was poking his head in the oven. It was such a shock that I still remember it clearly. It was the guy with the vegetable pushcart who sold his stuff to immigrant*

*families in the neighbourhood. He was an older man, with a big mustache and baggy pants. Mum would have nothing to do with the garlic seller, and I always stayed away from him, too—his long, hanging sausages frightened me! There in the kitchen, he made a face at my mother and said something in Italian. I don't know what he said, but it sounded like he was trying to explain something. He fished some things out of his pants pocket. I later learned it was a bulb of garlic and a couple of onions. At the time, she just stared at him, slack-jawed. Over the years, this story became part of the family lore—our best guess is that he smelled the turkey from the street and was telling Mum that the roast needed more flavour.*[1]

"Wasn't she a good cook?" I asked.

"Mum can do a pretty good lemon meringue pie when pressed, but she was more into her art and music than cooking. Sometimes she'd forget to put the dressing into a roast turkey. Mum's Canadian cooking meant lots of canned soup, cheese slices, bologna sandwiches, porridge and corn flakes. For her, exotic meant nutmeg."

I asked Kirk how their diet changed once she added the garlic and onions to the turkey. He laughed. "She never put it in. We never, ever ate onions or garlic. The very notion was repellent—we made faces and joked about bad breath and such. I ended up eating bland food until I left for university. Things could have been really different that day, but Mum stopped it, just in time."

Patricia Elliot's encounter with garlic may seem like small potatoes, but it represents a big change in Ontario's culture. Anglo-Canadians had always tried to keep up with the times and stay modern. But they still held on to centuries of prejudicial attitudes toward things like garlic. It was a battle fought over and over. Old Ontario won the battle but lost the war, eventually leading to a new culture that places foods like garlic at its forefront.

I wrote this book to trace the twisting path of garlic throughout Ontario's history, from exotica to pariah to its present-day status as a key part of our cuisine. I start with garlic's discovery by prehistoric humans—as an important food and medicine—in the Tien Shan mountains of central Asia. From there I'll lead you on a trip across the Eurasian continent as garlic spread along the ancient trails known as the Silk Road. I'll give you a peek at King Tut in ancient Egypt and some early settlements in northern Europe. We'll hitch a ride to the New World courtesy of the Vikings, and then I'll take you on a grand journey forward, all the way to present-day Ontario, where legend has it that Toronto's Transit Commission once had a rule making it illegal to ride a streetcar on a Sunday if you had been eating garlic.

# INTRODUCTION

To explain why it's been both loved and hated, I'll look at garlic as an object of cultural stereotypes and how perception can influence taste. Through stories such as "Mike Myers and the Garlic French Toast," I'll show why cooks used to hide it, lest people knew what they were eating, and I'll show you how to plant it—with a how-to guide for novice garlic gardeners. We'll also review the latest thinking on the medicinal uses of garlic, with hints on how to read between the lines when learning about the latest health benefit. I'll give you a look at the chemistry of garlic—why it tastes the way it does—with tips that will change forever how you use this versatile plant in your cuisine. Finally, to get you cooking with garlic, I'll offer forty recipes—both historical and contemporary—courtesy of some of Ontario's finest chefs. I'll also explain why you should keep buying local garlic.

Unplug your nose and get ready for a ride through the history of garlic as told by ancient travelers, Canadian settlers and early immigrants, farmers, professional chefs and newly converted garlic lovers. You'll never again look at a bulb of garlic the same way.

*Chapter 1*

# GARLIC IS IN A CLASS OF ITS OWN

*It amused us every time to watch him enjoy a curry made with garlic while at the same time holding such disdain for it.*

—*James Chatto*

Victorian writer John Ruskin called garlic a "strong class barrier"— good for labourers, but nothing that would be brought into a decent kitchen.[2] Similarly, Ontarians' perception of garlic's taste and smell was influenced by its associations. Let's look at a few examples of garlic being associated with a particular economic or social class in other countries. We'll also look at two other foods—lobster and tomatoes—that were reviled before they were loved.

Within Japan, the Ainu people (an indigenous group now centred in Hokkaido) were seen as inferior. Their consumption of *kitopiro* (wild garlic) was a symbol of "their perceived inferiority" compared to the dominant Japanese culture.[3] Another group, Japan's ethnic Korean minority, was frequently discriminated against and labeled with the derogatory term "garlic eaters" for their consumption of kimchi.

In 1930s Germany, garlic held negative connotations. For the Nazis, garlic was so indelibly associated with the Jewish population that "the mere mention of garlic by a Nazi orator caused the crowd to howl with fury."[4]

In North America, the association of garlic with immigrants was disseminated in cartoons, advertisements and Hollywood movies. One such cartoon, published in 1910, depicts a working-class Italian man shining the

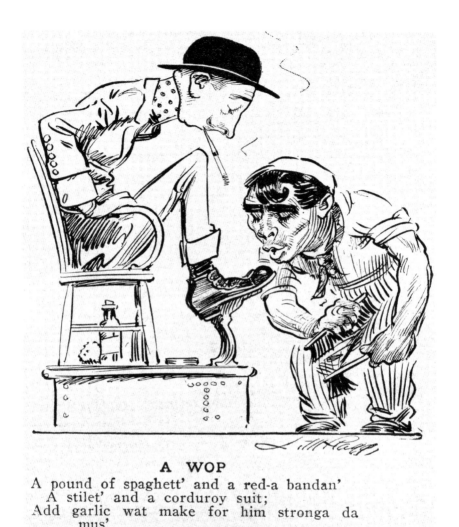

**A WOP**

A pound of spaghett' and a red-a bandan'
 A stilet' and a corduroy suit;
Add garlic wat make for him stronga da
    mus'
 And a talent for black-a da boot!

This 1910 cartoon associates garlic with immigrants in a negative tone. *Getty Images.*

shoe of a wealthy man in a bowler hat. Titled "A WOP," it included the following caption:

*A pound of spaghett' and a red-a bandan'*
*A stilet' and a corduroy suit;*
*Add garlic wat make for him stronga da mus'*
*And a talent for black-a da boot!*

A 1940s Kleenex ad associates garlic and germs with immigrants.

Although published in Chicago, the stereotype expressed in this illustration was also common in Canada at the time.[5]

A Kleenex advertisement from the 1940s sold the idea that tissues were invaluable tools in the fight against public germs. The caption read, "By putting a Kleenex over the mouthpiece when I talk on the public telephone… it helps me avoid catching germs while I'm catching my man!" And just who is infecting the indignant woman? Why, a man eating a green onion (one of garlic's cousins). With his exaggerated mustache, bushy eyebrows and darker complexion, he displays all the marks of a stereotypical immigrant.

In Frank Capra's classic 1946 film *It's a Wonderful Life*, actor Jimmy Stewart plays small-town banker George Bailey, a man who has great faith in the local immigrant population. He offers a loan to Mr. Martini, the owner of a local bar. The sinister Mr. Potter (played brilliantly by Lionel Barrymore) excoriates Bailey for providing a bank loan to an immigrant with no collateral—just his faith that Martini will honour the loan. Potter's prejudice is revealed when he imperiously tells the "do-gooder" Bailey that he is "frittering his life away playing nursemaid to a lot of garlic eaters."[6]

In Ontario, garlic was frequently associated with non-British foreigners. After Italy declared war on Britain, sentiment against Italian Canadians hardened. Italians working in Timmins faced physical threats and regular "registration lineups" by the Royal Canadian Mounted Police (RCMP). Leo Mascioli recounted a story: "One day, we were lined up to be fingerprinted, and a tall blond chap in front of me was whistling. The RCMP officer, who was twenty feet away, told him, 'Hey you, stop that whistling. I don't want to smell that garlic!'"[7]

Garlic is not the first food to face prejudice. At various points in history, some of our now favourite foods were once considered poisonous, dirty or déclassé. Two examples are tomatoes and lobster. Like garlic, the prejudice was unrelated to taste. And like garlic, they taste the same now as they always did. The changes are in our perception.

Today, the tomato is ubiquitous in traditional Italian cooking, but it took time to catch on. After its introduction to Italy in the mid-sixteenth century, the New World plant was initially unpopular. Because its vines grew close to the ground, its fruit was considered to be of "low" status. People also feared that it was toxic or inedible; they cultivated varieties of this "nightshade" fruit as ornamentals, not food. It was not until the nineteenth century that the tomato overcame its pariah status and began to be commonly eaten.[8]

Today, lobster is considered a luxury food, mentioned in the same breath as caviar and champagne. But this was not always the case. Until the mid-nineteenth century, North American lobster was a poor man's food on the East Coast, worth little more than pig feed. It was served to prisoners and not as a treat. Even domestic workers showed their dislike for lobster—they were known to request a limit of eating lobster no more than twice a week. The perception of lobster changed as the railways made their way inland. Railway managers started serving inexpensive lobster to their unwitting passengers. The passengers, in turn, were unaware of its low status. They could appreciate its delicious and subtle taste unfettered by negative associations. As its image improved, its price rose. A pound of lobster once sold for less than a pound of beans. Today, beans are one of the cheapest staples on the market, while lobster is considered a luxury item, affordable only as a special treat.

Food prejudices are not limited to social stigmas, as a study at Columbia Business School shows. In the study, subjects were given beer to drink. Control subjects drank unadulterated beer; a separate group tasted the same beer surreptitiously mixed with a few drops of balsamic vinegar. Both groups reported similarly favourable reactions to the taste. The experiment was repeated, but this time the second set of subjects was told in advance that it would be drinking beer with added vinegar.[9] I'll tell you the results at the end of the chapter.

Food prejudices can be deeply ingrained for some people, and in the case of garlic, if they knew it was in their food, they'd stop eating it. The following stories are reminiscent of Shakespeare's *Twelfth Night*. The play explores the complication of loving someone whose true identity is concealed. In the work, Viola, disguised as a man, does not want Olivia (who falls in love with her) to know her true identity. In the same way, garlic sometimes takes the role of Viola. Let's look at stories about garlic's hidden identity told in mid-nineteenth-century London, turn-of-the-century Paris and twentieth-century Canada.

Charles Elmé Francatelli was an Italian-born chef who was trained in France but spent most of his life in England. He eventually rose to the position of Queen Victoria's chief cook. But long before that, in 1850, he started as chef at the Reform Club in London. The Reform Club was intended as a forum for the more progressive members of both houses of Parliament. But they were not progressive enough to appreciate garlic. It was there that Francatelli prepared a salad in a most memorable way, flavouring it with the seldom-used plant. When a patron of the club asked about the salad's unusual and delicious taste, Francatelli revealed that the secret was garlic, but that's not all. Francatelli also told him that there was no actual garlic in the salad. Instead, he had crushed a clove in his teeth and breathed the garlicky vapours onto the salad. No doubt the patron was so taken aback by the chef's unusual method of preparation that he forgot he "hated" garlic. Across the channel, in Paris, Auguste Escoffier was more subtle. He contrived to include garlic in a dish he made just once a year for one of his more famous patrons, Sarah Bernhardt.

Bernhardt was the most famous actress of the nineteenth century and Escoffier the world's most famous chef. Once a year, on her birthday, he prepared her favourite dish: his scrambled eggs. His ingredients were simple, but his method was sublime. He slow-cooked it over low heat for half an hour while stirring it in a *bain marie* (double boiler). This ensured well-aerated eggs, more like a custard in texture than a simple scramble. He never revealed his secret flavour, though: Escoffier stirred the eggs with a clove of garlic pinned on a fork. He realized that if Bernhardt, a self-described garlic hater, knew his secret, she'd never again eat his eggs, so Escoffier held his garlic close to his chest for all the years he knew her.[10]

Farmers' market manager Cookie Roscoe told a story of her unique French toast. It was around the time, in the mid-1980s, that she first heard about a recipe for chicken with forty cloves of garlic. "It seemed revolutionary." Maybe that inspired her when her friend Mike Myers visited. Says Roscoe, "I was living in Winnipeg and Myers came by after a show. He was in the Second City touring company, and all I had in the house was a loaf of stale bread and some eggs. So I dressed it up by adding a little garlic powder. Since Myers was still a bashful kid from Scarborough, garlic was an unrecognizable and exotic ingredient."[11] Myers may not have liked or known about the garlic, but he sure liked Roscoe's French toast. Her recipe wasn't as crazy as it seems. Years later, Magic Oven's Garlic French Toast with Fruit Compote and Crème Fraîche proved to be a crowd pleaser at the 2013 and 2014 Toronto Garlic Festival (see image in the color section).

Toronto food writer James Chatto told of an intriguing love/hate relationship with garlic. He recalled how his British father hated garlic but loved curry, which sometimes was made with garlic. "He never included garlic as an ingredient when he made his own curry, but when he ate curry made by others, he liked the taste, even though he knew there was garlic in it. My family would teasingly remind him of the ingredients…turmeric, cumin, ginger, cardamom…garlic. It amused us every time to watch him enjoy a curry made with garlic while at the same time holding such disdain for it."[12]

These stories point to something interesting: garlic has such strong negative associations that it precludes some people from appreciating its taste. It's not surprising that subjects in the Columbia Business School study who were told of the vinegar before they drank the beer had a negative reaction to the taste. Their anticipation affected their flavour perception—an offensive idea led to a bad taste. Why does knowing about the vinegar before tasting the beer influence the outcome? Why wouldn't Sarah Bernhardt have eaten Escoffier's eggs if she'd known they were cooked with garlic? And how is this connected to historical prejudices toward garlic? The answer lies in understanding the role of taste and flavour in human evolution.

Humans taste food using thousands of receptor cells on the tongue. The sensation of taste is made up of five categories: sweet, sour, salt, bitter and umami. This information is conveyed to the brain along with other factors, including texture, temperature, coolness, heat and, most important, the sense of smell. The totality of these sensory inputs, along with memories and associations, is what constitutes the flavour of a food item.

In early humans, the ability to form memories associated with taste served a different purpose than it does today. In hunter-gatherer cultures, a sweet-tasting food meant high sugar. High sugar meant high energy, and this offered a better chance for survival. A bitter taste signaled a potential poison. Sweetness meant life, while bitterness meant death. The ability to remember a sweet-tasting berry versus a bitter-tasting plant helped ensure our survival.[13]

Jump ahead a few thousand years to modern civilization. The ability to make associations and form memories around a taste or smell took on a different purpose. As humans divided into strata according to economic or social criteria, a system evolved to mark these classes. British social classes, for example, were distinguished largely through language and pronunciation. A person's social status could be determined from childhood by his accent. Pronunciation as a class marker exists in many places in the world, even in Ontario. In nineteenth-century Toronto, Spadina House was pronounced "spa-dee-na" by well-heeled, mostly Anglo-Torontonians north of Bloor.[14] It was pronounced "spa-dye-na" by the immigrant population to its south, largely Italians, Jews, Poles and Ukrainians. What further distinguished these Europeans from their neighbours north of Bloor? For the most part they were garlic eaters.

## Chapter 2

# THE FIRST TASTE

*She nibbled on a clove to taste it and was surprised by a curious heat sensation.*
*It burned her tongue.*

It's believed that garlic was first discovered thousands of years ago in central Asia.[15] We have valued the root ever since. How did it all begin? One imagined scenario is that about ten thousand years ago (or possibly earlier), a few hunter-gatherer women were walking along a hillside. They lived among the Tien Shan Mountains, in part of the "Garlic Crescent."[16] They wore animal skins and clothes made from plant fibres and fed themselves by foraging for nuts, berries and eggs while keeping an eye on the young children who accompanied them. One of them pulled some bulbs of garlic from the soil. *Were they safe to eat? Would they be useful for survival…or poisonous?* She sniffed it and noticed that it smelled similar to related plants she had eaten. She hadn't been sick then, so these were probably edible, too. She kept them. On the way back, she noticed that, unlike the berries and fruit they were carrying, no insects crawled on the garlic. It seemed to have strong powers. Perhaps it could fight illnesses.[17] She nibbled on a clove to taste it and was surprised by a curious heat sensation. It burned her tongue.

Back at their makeshift camp, she cooked the bulb over burning embers. They all licked their lips at the pleasant aroma it emitted and gobbled up its sweet, caramel flavour. Sweet foods were a rare treat. News of its valuable benefits would pass from tribe to tribe, from generation to generation. Later, garlic became a valuable trading commodity, along with spices, obsidian,

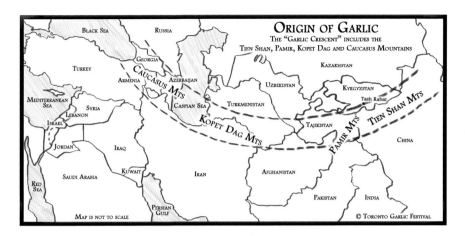

Garlic is believed to have originated in the "Garlic Crescent," most likely in the Tien Shan Mountains. *Courtesy of Toronto Garlic Festival.*

seashells, precious stones and other high-value materials. Over the centuries it became an important plant used as food, preservative, medicine and ritual ingredient in spiritual and religious practices.

By 6000 BCE, garlic had traveled thousands of miles from its point of origin.[18] Garlic remains from 6,000 years ago have been found in the Cave of the Treasure, near Ein Gedi, Israel,[19] and garlic-shaped clay artifacts from 5,800 years ago were discovered in a tomb at El Mahasna, Egypt.[20] Garlic was also mentioned in the Bible and the Quran.[21] The earliest known evidence of an allium plant used as a flavouring comes from 6,000-year-old pottery shards found in modern-day Denmark and Germany. The shards contained silicate remains of garlic mustard (*Alliaria petiolata*), as well as animal and fish residues. It confirms that Mesolithic and early Neolithic hunter-gatherers ate plants not simply as a means of sustaining themselves.[22] Indeed, one of the earliest recorded recipes using garlic is from the Yale Babylonian tablets dated from 1700 to 1600 BCE. These small clay tablets contain forty recipes, one of which, for meat pie, requires pounding together leek and garlic.[23]

From its origin in the Garlic Crescent, how did garlic travel across Eurasia and eventually to the farms and gardens in Ontario some ten thousand years later? The answer lies in the nature of garlic and the geography of its origin.

The Garlic Crescent was in the centre of what came to be the marauding and trading crossroads of ancient Eurasia. There were a limited number of east–west routes from China to the Mediterranean and between Asia's north and south. Many routes led along the valleys and mountain passes of the

Garlic Crescent. Later, the trade of garlic accelerated with the development of the ancient Silk Road more than two thousand years ago. Traders and pilgrims moved with relative ease between markets in Asia, India, the Levant, southern Europe and northern Africa, spreading information and goods along the way. To ensure the safety of travelers hundreds of caravanserai (from the Persian word *caravan*, meaning group of people and animals traveling on a long journey, and *serai*, a place to stay) were built along the routes.[24]

At an elevation of 3,500 metres (11,480 feet), the caravanserai at Tash Rabat sits in southern Kyrgyzstan on the north side of the Tien Shan. It is one of the best-preserved monuments to the Silk Road. From as early as the fifteenth century CE, its stone walls sheltered traders from bandits and the harsh mountain weather.[25] The high ceilings accommodated the traders as well as their animals. A local traveler might trade a few bulbs of garlic for one or two seashells carried by the leader of a camel caravan from eastern China.

On the southern slope of the Tien Shan Mountains, the Kashgar market (in Xinjiang Province, China) was the major trading post between China and trading partners to the west. In 1399, Marco Polo wrote about Kashgar in the way a trade conference might be described today. "This country is the starting point from which many merchants set out to market their wares all over the world."[26] Many items Marco Polo saw and smelled are still available in Kashgar today: sheep and cattle at the livestock market, carpets, pottery, fruit and vegetables…and garlic. Two thousand years after its start, the Kashgar market is still open for business.[27]

Places like the caravanserai at Tash Rabat and the market in Kashgar were located, by happy coincidence, at the very heart of garlic's origin. This proximity helped spur the trade of garlic far and wide. I went there myself, somewhat fortuitously, in 2008 on a trip through eastern China, Uzbekistan, Kazakhstan and Kyrgyzstan. If only I had been in Tash Rabat a few years later, after I had kindled my love of garlic! I would have appreciated the place in a different way.

After I got to know garlic grower Bob Litke, I told him that I had visited Tien Shan. His eyes lit up, like a devout Christian meeting someone who had touched the Holy Grail.

"How much garlic did you bring back?"

"None. I didn't know about garlic's connection to Tien Shan back then."

He replied instantly: "Idiot!"

There is a second reason garlic migrated easily across Eurasia: it could grow almost anywhere. Thanks to its hardy nature, almost everywhere

*Right*: The caravanserai at Tash Rabat is one of the best-preserved monuments of the ancient Silk Road. *Photo by Peter McClusky.*

*Below*: The author, Peter McClusky, inside the main room of the caravanserai at Tash Rabat. *Photo by Peter McClusky.*

garlic was traded, it was planted. This may account for why garlic was not as commercially valuable as other spices, such as cinnamon, nutmeg, caccia and pepper. The supply of these spices could be controlled, either by keeping their source a secret or because they could not be replanted easily. This is what made Kerala province, in India, one of the busiest trading ports in ancient Asia.

Vasco da Gama was the first European to reach Asia by sea; he landed in Kerala in 1498 and loaded his ship with precious peppers. He asked the traders if he could take a whole pepper stalk on his return voyage to Portugal, to replant. Legend has it that the savvy traders' instinct to protect their tightly controlled supply gave way to the realization that the plants would not grow well away from the soil and climate of Kerala Province. Their reply: "Yes, you can take our peppers, but you will never be able to take our rains."[28] Not so with garlic. The plant thrived in a relatively wide range of soil conditions and climates.

Toronto chef Sanjiz Mathews tells the story of how the pepper trade first drew his ancestors to Kerala, seventeen centuries ago. They emigrated from southern Mesopotamia to Cranganore on the Malabar coast in present-day Kerala Province. They were involved in the spice trade. Centuries later, Mathews's family moved with their recipes to Canada. He carries on his family's tradition of spice trader, selling his specialty spice mix at Toronto's farmers' markets. He's also famous for his garlic chutney. Mathews's story is one of many examples of how the ancient Asian trade routes, and garlic, extended not just across thousands of miles but over the centuries, all the way to Ontario.

But garlic had already taken a different route to the New World.

*Chapter 3*
# THE NEW WORLD

*The fact that Worcestershire sauce was promoted for medicinal purposes*
*gave license to the generous use of garlic.*

In 1000 CE, Viking explorer Leif Eriksson touched down in L'Anse aux Meadows on the northern tip of Newfoundland. And with him came garlic. Garlic had had a nine-thousand-year head start in Eurasia and Africa, but Lucky Leif brought the first bulbs to North America.[29] It was thought to give strength and courage and had a reputation for adapting to different soil and climate conditions.[30] This is probably why he chose to bring it on his voyage from Greenland. He didn't know that various allium species were already growing wild in North America.

*Allium tricoccum*—commonly known as ramps, wild leek or wild garlic—was found in most of eastern North America, including Ontario. These plants have a flavour and odour similar to garlic and onion. Explorer Robert de la Salle mentioned an area, south of present-day Ontario, where local natives said the plant grew in abundance. In 1687, De la Salle described the Algonquin name *Che-ka-kou* as a "place of the smelly onions." Today's Chicago (Toronto's sister city) was built on that site.[31]

Another plant native to North America is *Allium canadense*. Also known as Canada onion, wild garlic and Canada garlic, it predates Leif Eriksson's visit.[32] Various First Nations peoples used the plant as a medicine. They rubbed it on their bodies for protection against insect and animal bites.[33]

The plant was also eaten. The Iroquois of Lake Ontario ate the bulbs and greens cooked in soups or raw.[34]

Natives and French settlers shared a liking for "Anonque," a wild garlic with a particularly strong smell. In 1632, Gabriel Sagard recorded that both groups favoured the plant, but not when they smelled it on the other: "[W]hen we had eaten some of these onions or garlic raw, as we did when we had nothing else, along with a little purslane, but no bread, the savages would not come near us nor bear the odour of our breath, declaring that it smelt too bad, and they would spit on the ground with disgust."[35]

Garlic had an auspicious start in the early days of the settlers in Canada. It was an ingredient in the first gastronomic society in North America. L'Ordre de Bon Temps (the Order of Good Cheer) was launched at Port Royal, Nova Scotia, during the winter of 1606–7 by French explorer Samuel de Champlain. Champlain's intent was to improve the health and good cheer of his men in the harsh winter by providing a regular gathering that served locally prepared fare. Men, women and children from nearby First Nations groups were invited to the feast. Members took turns serving as the designated "Chief Steward," going hunting and fishing for two days to gather food for the upcoming feast (see Jeffreys painting in the color section). They brought back birds including mallards, geese and partridges, as well as animals like moose, caribou, beaver, otter, bear, rabbit, wildcat and raccoon.[36]

At the start of the feast, the Chief Steward marched in, napkin on his shoulder, badge of office in his hand and the collar of the Order around his neck. He was followed by the members, each carrying a dish. In his fictionalized account, writer Bill Gaston reimagines a scene from the Order, including a member, Marc Lescarbot, as the Chief Steward: "Lescarbot's night went well, despite the lawyer taking every opportunity to describe, in verse, each dish as it got carried to the table. But there was a fine beaver tail made in a pie, with such addition of garlic and salt and butter that it could have been as exquisite as aspic of escargot."[37]

The party did not last long. After years of checks and counterchecks between the French and British, it all ended at the Plains of Abraham (1759). The French were placed under British rule. Outside Quebec, a lid was placed on cooking with garlic. The use of garlic in cooking followed the political map.

The French grew garlic to eat. Hugh Murray's *The Enyclopaedia of Geography* (1837) recounts his observations along the St. Lawrence. In a tour of Lower Canada (modern-day Quebec), he reported a chain of farms more than forty miles long. "The French habitans have an extremely imperfect mode of culture…culinary vegetables are raised in tolerable plenty, especially onions, garlic, and leeks."

The British used garlic more than they appeared to. This is important when looking at Upper Canada's (modern-day Ontario) use of garlic. Even when they were at war with the French, the British weren't averse to French culture—including clothing, fashion and cuisine. French politics played a role in this. After the French Revolution in 1789 and political instability in the early nineteenth century, many aristocrats fled Paris. Their French-trained chefs relocated to London, garlic in hand. Given this influence, the staff at Historic Fort York believe that garlic may have been grown for pickling, sauces and medicinal use in the garden at Fort York in the nineteenth century.[38] A recipe, "To Dress Eggs with Garlic," from *La Cuisinière Bourgeoise* (1746), a very popular French cookbook in its English translation, was recently re-created at the fort (see the original recipe and the modern equivalent on page 131).

However, the path from medicine cabinet to cooking pot was a slow one and limited to certain types of condiments and cooking. British explorer, writer and linguist Sir Richard Burton credited garlic for the success of Worcestershire sauce, "whose fortune was made by the nice conduct of garlic."[39] The appreciation of garlic in this sauce also reached Canada. The July 1872 issue of *Canada Presbyterian* (in the "Scientific and Useful" column) provided a recipe for Worcestershire sauce and recommended to add "a sufficient quantity of crushed garlic…to give it a decided garlic taste."[40]

Melissa Beynon planting garlic in historic dress at Fort York National Historic Site. *Photo by Peter McClusky.*

THE

## COOK NOT MAD;

OR

## RATIONAL COOKERY:

BEING

A COLLECTION OF ORIGINAL AND SELECT

### RECEIPTS,

Embracing not only the art of curing various
kinds of Meats and Vegetables for future
use, but of Cooking, in its general
acceptation, to the taste, habits,
and degrees of luxury, pre-
valent with the

### CANADIAN PUBLIC,

TO WHICH ARE ADDED,

Directions for preparing comforts for the S...
Room—together with sundry miscellaneous
kinds of information, of importance to house-
keepers in general, nearly all tested by
experience.

KINGSTON, U. C.
Published by James Macfarlane.
1831.

THE

## FRUGAL HOUSEWIFE'S MANUAL:

CONTAINING

### A NUMBER OF USEFUL RECEIPTS,

CAREFULLY SELECTED, AND WELL ADAPTED TO THE USE
OF FAMILIES IN GENERAL.

To which are added

### PLAIN AND PRACTICAL DIRECTIONS

FOR THE

CULTIVATION AND MANAGEMENT OF SOME OF THE MOST USEFUL

### CULINARY VEGETABLES.

BY A. B., OF GRIMSBY

Toronto:
Guardian Office, No. 9, Wellington Buildings.
J. H. LAWRENCE, PRINTER.
1840.

THE

## FEMALE EMIGRANT'S

## GUIDE,

AND

## Hints on Canadian Housekeeping.

BY MRS. C. P. TRAILL,

AUTHORESS OF THE "BACKWOODS OF CANADA," "FOREST
GLEANINGS," "THE CANADIAN CRUSOES," &c., &c.

SECOND THOUSAND.

TORONTO, C. W:
SOLD BY MACLEAR AND COMPANY,
AND ALL THE PRINCIPAL BOOKSELLERS THROUGHOUT CANADA, THE
BRITISH AMERICAN PROVINCES, AND THE UNITED STATES.
1854.

Price Twenty-Five Cents, or One Shilling and Three-pence, each part,
postpaid to any part of Canada, the British American Provinces,
and the United States.

*Above, left*: *The Cook Not Mad, or Rational Cookery*
(1831) was the first cookbook published in
Canada. *Courtesy of Baldwin Collection of Canadiana.*

*Above, right*: *The Frugal Housewife's Manual* (1840)
was the first cookbook compiled in Canada.
*Courtesy of Baldwin Collection of Canadiana.*

*Left*: *The Female Emigrant's Guide* (1854)
was intended as an orientation on food
preparation for English immigrants. *Courtesy
of Baldwin Collection of Canadiana.*

The fact that Worcestershire sauce was promoted for medicinal purposes gave license to the generous use of garlic.

David Beaton, a Scot, was one of the earliest naval officers on Lake Ontario. He carried Lieutenant Governor Simcoe on his first voyage to Niagara in 1792. His wife, Sarah Beaton, recorded her cure for whooping cough: "Take an equal quantity of hog's lard and garlic, pounded together, and rub the back bone, the soles of the feet and palms of the hands every night going to bed."

Thus, garlic was used but not ubiquitously. Three important nineteenth-century cookbooks in Upper Canada made little or no mention of garlic. *The Cook Not Mad* (1831) was the first cookbook published in Canada. It was an edition of a work from New York, with recipes that derived from Anglo-American tastes.[41] Along with cooking recipes, it included expert advice on a miscellany of topics, such as "[H]ow to expel nameless intruders from children's heads...Steep larkspur seed in water, rub the liquor a few times into the child's hair, and the business of destruction is done." While onions are called for in several recipes, including a recipe for Beef Steak Pie, not one recipe in the book calls for garlic. The closest reference to garlic is a section on how to store onions and "other bulbous roots."[42]

*The Frugal Housewife's Manual* (1840) was the first English-language cookbook compiled in Canada, with some recipes taken from earlier British and American cookbooks.[43] None of the recipes calls for garlic as an ingredient.

*The Female Emigrant's Guide* (1854) set out to acclimate British immigrant women to this strange new world. The only reference to garlic is to wild garlic, "dreaded by the dairy-made as it destroys the flavour of the milk and spoils the butter."[44]

*Household Recipes or Domestic Cookery* (1865) was written specifically for the Canadian kitchen.[45] It calls for garlic in two recipes: Stewed Fish Brown Sauce and a recipe for Stewed Veal, which daringly calls for "a garlic chopped fine."[46]

The rare recipes that called for garlic did so apologetically—measured in fractions or, if a whole clove is used, boiled or cooked whole. While garlic was a much-used ingredient in tonics and condiments, in the kitchen it was often muted or simply not called for in recipes.

## Chapter 4
# GARLIC

## OUI OR NO?

*You can't marry a garlic eater.*
—*Elizabeth and Herbert Parry*

In the nineteenth century, British imperial power was at its height, with Victorian pink seen everywhere on world maps. Canada was still pink and part of the empire. In 1867, Upper and Lower Canada, Nova Scotia and New Brunswick decided to confederate into a new country. The Dominion of Canada was born, with Ontario (Upper Canada) becoming the centre of its English-speaking population. It was a new nation steeped in old British cultural attitudes.

As it felt its way across the continent, Canada brimmed with a newfound optimism. Immigrants poured in, both from Great Britain and from across its empire, with people of Chinese, South Asian and African origins joining those from the British Isles.[47] Americans, too, looked to the north and west, with many settling in Canada. And non-British Europeans saw Canada as one of the few unexplored frontiers. Joining the Irish and German migrants, Swedes, Italians, Jews, Ukrainians, Mennonites, Poles and many others looked at Canada as the best place to live. As Wilfrid Laurier wrote in 1904, "the Twentieth Century will be the Century of Canada."[48]

By 1900, Ontario was still very much an English-dominated society, with Toronto overwhelmingly British.[49] In the east and the north, Franco-Ontarians held on to their garlic-rich cuisines, cooking their tourtiere with garlic and onion. Garlic played a smaller role in Anglo-Ontario. Immigrants were assimilated to fit in to the British norm, but in their own homes, out of the public eye, they continued to cook with garlic.

Early on, garlic appeared to make headway in Anglo-Ontario. In addition to its medicinal use, some food recipes called for large amounts of garlic. Some people even considered garlic an "upper-class" flavour. In 1897, the *Evening Star*, the predecessor of the *Toronto Star*, ran a story in its Saturday edition on "Curries and Rice." "Only those men and women who have lived in luxury under the suns of the tropics understand thoroughly how to set a summer table." The article describes a "Genuine East Indian Chicken Curry" and its directions do not stint on spices. These included coriander seed, turmeric, black pepper, mustard, ginger, cardamom seed, cumin seed and cayenne pepper. Even garlic is mentioned, if cautiously. Garlic is "not strictly necessary."[50]

The best-selling Canadian cookbook, and the first community cookbook of the nineteenth century, is *The Home Cook Book*.[51] Almost four hundred pages of the 1887 edition contain five recipes calling for garlic: Worcester Sauce,[52] Tomato "Catsup,"[53] Stewed Tongue,[54] Beef Cakes[55] and English Sauce.[56]

Anglo-Ontarians ruled. The more British you seemed, the higher your status, while "un-British" types were perceived as lower class. With few exceptions, non-British immigrants used garlic. Canadians known to eat garlic were identified as immigrants or foreigners. This embarrassment brought alienation and feelings of being the "other." Until well past World War II, garlic eaters "knew what we were," said Helena Moroz, reflecting on the relationship of garlic to her ethnicity. "We were associated with the ethnic populations. No self-respecting Anglo would participate."[57]

Ironically, it was a foreign influence that elevated garlic's status. But that worked only as long as the foreign influence did not arrive on Canadian soil. For Canadians at the time, India was a part of the British empire… and far away. Garlic was considered "exotic" by some. But the flirtation was fleeting. When immigrants began to arrive from around the world in increasing numbers, garlic's association with "poor" or "backward" people became cemented.

Attitudes toward garlic followed Canadians traveling abroad. Miss Helen J. Melville was a Canadian missionary. She wrote of her trip to Kamundongo in German east Africa (present-day Rwanda) in the *Monthly Leaflet of the Canada Congregational Woman's Board of Mission* (December 1897). She mentions a meal sent by a local chief in Kamundongo: "The chicken was nicely cooked, except that it had garlic in it which we do not like."[58] Notice her use of the word *we*. It suggests an institutional dislike of garlic.

But garlic was being consumed in Ontario, and not only by non-British. Mouthwash advertisements, plays and memoranda to dentists were all indications that there were secret garlic eaters. An amusing play written in the early twentieth century shows how garlic was at the crossroads of culture. The play was written by members of the Mooradian family. Yeghishe Mooradian came to Canada in 1906 from the village of Arek in Keghi in the province of Erzeroum, Armenia. He established a small business in Brantford and soon brought other family members over. The Mooradian family went to great lengths to preserve their culture, studying the Armenian language, both reading and writing, as well as writing plays. One work, by brother and sister playwrights Alexander and Francis Mooradian, preserves the dialect of pre–World War I Keghi. In the following excerpt, a young boy, Arsen, escorts his sixty-five-year-old Armenian-speaking grandmother, Sara, to a dental appointment. The dentist almost collapses from the strong smell of garlic on her breath, although she insists that she hasn't eaten garlic. The difficulties of translation become more comical as the scene progresses:

*Dentist: My God, my God, it smells terribly.*
*Sara: (in Armenian) Ask the doctor what happened that he is crying for God. Is he going to fix my tooth or not, for Heaven's sake?*
*Arsen: My grandmother wants to know why you cried out, my God, my God?*
*Dentist: Why? Can't you smell the garlic?*
*Arsen: Grandma, doctor says you have eaten garlic.*
*Sara: (annoyed and knitting her eyebrows) Col'blimey, tell the doctor I have not eaten garlic. I've eaten pacha. P A C H A.*
*Arsen: (very faithfully) Doctor, my grandma says she has not eaten garlic, but pacha.*
*Dentist: (bending toward Arsen) What?*
*Arsen: (louder) Pacha! P A C H A!*
*Dentist: How do you spell it?*
*Arsen: I don't know. (To his grandmother in Armenian) The doctor asks how you "spell" pacha. [Here Arsen, not knowing the Armenian word for "spell," uses the English word instead.]*
*Sara: Goodness gracious! Does the doctor want to know how to cook pacha?*
*Arsen: (a little annoyed) No grandma. No, (Armenian) S P E L L, S P E L L.*
*Sara: Kah, goodness, what's "spell"? I said pacha.*
*Arsen: Oh no.*
*Dentist: (interested) What are you talking about?*

*Arsen: She cannot spell it.*

*Dentist: Then ask her what is it.*

*Arsen: Grandma, the doctor wants to know what pacha is.*

*Sara: (wringing her hands and with a loud voice) What pacha is?...(To the doctor in Armenian) Pity your good looks [idiom]. How could you be a grown man and with all your education...(To Arsen in Armenian) Heavens, tell the gentleman that pacha is food and not clothing. It's pig's feet, pig's head, goat's feet, goat's brains, cow's feet, cow's brains. We mix them all together. We put them in a big pot, cover it and we cook it and cook it until it cooks real good, when it cooks...Then we add garlic and fenugreek and then we have pacha. Tell him. Tell him how I told you. Maybe he wants to eat it and he doesn't know how to cook it.*

*Arsen: (a little confused as to how to explain all this) Doctor, grandma says pacha is nice food. You know, lamb's head, lamb's feet, goat's head, goat's feet, cow's head, cow's feet. Mix some garlic with it, it makes a nice, nice thing to eat. And that is what they call pacha.*

*Dentist: Is that so?*

*Sara: (in Armenian) Tell him that I made some yesterday with my own hands. The doctor would eat his fingers with it.*

*Arsen: My grandma says if she cooks the pacha for you, you will eat your fingers with it.*

*Dentist: I will eat my fingers? No, no...What do you think? I am crazy?[59]*

It wasn't just the patients who ate garlic, but dentists themselves. The *Dominion Dental Journal* (1892) recommended dentists chew parsley to get rid of garlic breath.[60] Publications like the *Journal of Agriculture and Horticulture* (1898) touted garlic for its health benefits. "Leeks, Onions-Garlic and Shallots stimulate the circulation of the blood and promote digestion."[61] Another journal provided directions on garlic consumption, as if it were a prescription medicine dispensed by a pharmacist: "Garlic may be given in the form of powder, in capsules in 3 to 10 grains, or in the form of the *syrupus allii* (U.S.P.), in doses of 1 to 4 drachms."[62] However, garlic continued to be stigmatized as undesirable, immoral or even dangerous. In *Catechism of Hygiene for the Use of Convents and Female Schools*, an 1891 pamphlet for girls, the author cautioned against culinary excess: "We should take food not for pleasure, but through necessity." And on the question of condiments, including garlic, the pamphlet noted that "abuse of condiments gives rise to inflammation of the stomach which is very often fatal. Excess in all things indicates a sketch of madness."[63]

Ideas were often based on centuries-old writings. In the *Dominion Medical Monthly* (Toronto, 1915), a letter to the editor quoted sixteenth-century writers on the medical virtues of garlic. The letter also illustrates Ontarians' ongoing love-hate relationship with garlic. It refers to its delicious taste but warned that it is better appreciated if it isn't seen. "Sure I am our palate people are much pleased therewith as giving a delicious haut-gout to most meats they eat, as tasted and smelt in their sauce, though not seen therein."[64]

Canadians found their garlic in a variety of places. Some was imported from places like Italy. By 1900, Naples was the embarkation point for cheese, olive oil, macaroni and garlic sent to flourishing Italian communities abroad.[65] By this time, there were already eleven thousand Italians living in Canada, mostly in Montreal and Toronto.

Government officials encouraged garlic growing. A government-sponsored exhibit in 1901 of products grown in Northern Ontario, from Nipissing to the Rainy River Valley, includes raspberries, apples, tobacco and garlic.[66] Indeed, present-day garlic farmers testify to how suitable it is to the Northern Ontario climate.

Canada's first gardening guide, *The Canadian Fruit, Flower and Kitchen Gardener*, mentions garlic. Published in 1872, garlic's inclusion is based on the author's correspondence with horticulturalists in the provinces about fruits and vegetables best suited to the Canadian climate. Admittedly, garlic gets short shrift compared to other vegetables in the book. He advised (incorrectly, by modern standards) to plant it in April or May. Still, his description of how to use garlic was a step above most contemporaries: "It is used to flavor soups and stews, having an intense onion flavor."[67]

Immigrants from eastern and southern Europe and Asia brought their own garlic bulbs with them to plant. The tradition of carrying seeds to a new home had gone on for thousands of years. It's how garlic was disseminated, via trade and migration, from its origin in central Asia. Certain cultures, such as the Ukrainians, came from a land with a history of famine and starvation.[68] It was a survival strategy to bring seeds, including garlic. Pierre Berton recounted one such experience in *The Promised Land*:

> *It is a spring morning in 1897, and in the Galician village of Ghermakivka the Humenink family is packing to leave for Canada on money borrowed from relatives and friends. Everything they own takes up no more than twenty cubic feet and will be carefully stored away in a green wooden trunk built by Nykola Humeniuk himself. His wife, Anastasia, puts the winter clothes, blankets, and bed sheets at the bottom; next come the holy pictures, packed between pillows;*

*and on top of that the family's dress clothes for Sunday church (for surely there will be a little church with an onion-shaped spire in whatever community they reach). Then another covering, and twenty-five little cloth bundles of garden seeds—onions, garlic, horseradish, dried ears of corn—and above that some religious articles.*[69]

Some immigrants brought more than just garlic bulbs. There were tools like the garlic masher. Mary Stefura still has the wooden garlic masher that her grandmother, Irene Sykos, brought from the Ukraine in 1922. "She'd grasp it by the narrow end and mashed the garlic against a wood board."[70]

Sandra Sharko, a garlic grower, described how her father-in-law treasured the garlic he grew from the bulbs he brought from the Ukraine when he came to Canada in the early 1900s. "He worked in the mines in Sudbury. He was a garlic eater; he probably smelled of it and was made fun of for his love of garlic, but he was a prankster. One time he put a clove of garlic into the coat lining of one of his fellow miners." He shared his garlic with friends. Later, Sandra and her husband, Mike, grew it for about forty years, until they switched to the Music strain. They carried on the practice of sharing garlic with friends and strangers, who would plant it in their gardens. Said Sharko, who lives in Sudbury, "There's lots of garlic growing in backyards in Sudbury, more than you'd ever believe."[71]

Wooden garlic masher brought from Ukraine in 1922 by Irene Sukos. *Photo by Peter McClusky.*

This is confirmed by Stefura. She doesn't recall if her grandmother brought garlic over with the masher, but like many immigrants, she grew garlic in the family garden. Her grandfather arrived from the Ukraine in 1914 and opened a grocery store, Sykos' Grocery, in Espanola, Ontario. "Even though many of his customers were Polish and Ukrainian, he didn't sell garlic—his customers all grew garlic in their gardens."[72] In the Ukrainian community, just like in every community that used it, garlic existed as a kind of culinary "fifth column" within Ontario cuisine. Garlic was kept hidden, and when it did appear, it was driven back into the shadows.

In 1928, a meeting of the trustees and teachers for a school near Sudbury debated whether students who smelled of garlic could be admitted to class. "The question of whether or not we could send pupils home if they ate garlic, arose. It was decided that we could."[73] This was not an isolated incident. Jean Gural, who attended a religious school in Norfolk County in the early 1940s, remembered a similar experience in which she was given a garlic-related ultimatum: "In the town of Boston, Ontario (now called Waterford), the school I attended brought in spiritual singers. I wanted to attend Sunday school so I could participate. My parents were farmers; they never got dressed up. It was a chance for me to wear a dress and fancy hat and carry a purse. But there was a problem. My Sunday school teacher—I can't remember her name, she was prim and proper, well dressed—said to me, 'Jean, don't eat garlic if you come to Sunday school.'" Gural refrained from eating garlic on Sundays.

Gural described an annual event that brought together everyone in the community, though it might still have lacked community spirit. "During the wheat harvest a machine was used to thresh the wheat. It required that all the farmers work together, and even the meals were prepared communally, with each family taking a turn. When it was my mother's turn, it would be something the other farmers would like—roast chicken, mashed potatoes and vegetables, and elderberry pie. There wouldn't be any garlic." And when it was the neighbours' turn? "The same, it would always be their cooking—never Ukrainian, never garlic."[74]

Although these stories are from Ukrainians, they're mirrored in tales from other immigrants and descendants of immigrants. As Mike Murakami remembers, for many children of immigrants, bringing their mother's food to school would be "the first and last time." His own mother learned this. In 1925, his mother grew up in Victoria. She lived among the Chinese community and acquired a taste for Chinese snacks, including beetles preserved in salt. She took them to school and got kicked out of class.[75]

The pattern of immigrant children coming home crying, or just with hurt feelings, has lessened but not abated.[76]

Polish immigrant Mendel Shapiro came to garlic's defense on a white horse, and was firmly rebuffed. Sara Waxman, his daughter, told how her father ate raw garlic every day while serving with the Polish Red Army in the 1930s. "Every morning, the soldiers would receive a generous ration of garlic...to ward off illnesses like cold and flu. My father continued this practice, and many years later, here in Canada, he even attempted to get his daughters to participate. To his chagrin, we adamantly refused. We did, however, convince him to chew parsley immediately after chewing the garlic. The interesting thing is, I cannot recall him ever having a cold."[77]

Cultures collided with increasing frequency. Cookie Roscoe tells the story of when her parents, Nicholas Yarashko and Helen Parry, were

Mendel Shapiro, on the white horse, served in the Polish Red Army, mid-1930s. *Courtesy of Sara Waxman.*

*Left to right*: Stephan and Maria Yarashko, groom and bride Nicholas and Helen, and Elizabeth and Herbert Parry, Winnipeg, 1956. *Courtesy of Helen Roscoe.*

engaged to be married. The news was not well received by Helen's parents. Nicholas's parents were Ukrainian, while Helen's parents were British. They were at opposite ends of the garlic continuum. Nicholas ate garlic and the Parrys didn't. In voicing their objection to the marriage, young Helen's parents demanded, "You can't marry a garlic eater."[78]

But garlic was on the rise, culturally if not genetically. Young Helen married Nicholas, the garlic eater. One of their children, Cookie Roscoe, a garlic eater, married Kevin Frank, also a garlic eater. Cookie and Kevin had two children, both garlic eaters. What happens when you cross a garlic eater with a non-garlic eater? Their children are almost invariably garlic eaters. Still, vestiges of the old British attitude persisted. When Cookie's first daughter was a few weeks old, her mother warned, "I can smell garlic on that baby's breath."

*Chapter 5*
# GARLIC RISING

*Upon arriving home, before both feet were in the door, my wife could smell the garlic. "You've been to Carman's," she'd call out.*

—*Harry Rosen*

By the end of World War II, Canada had the fourth-largest armed forces in the world. The soldiers were coming home with a newfound exuberance. They had been exposed to languages, ideas and brand-new flavours. Back home, they made up for lost time and started to have kids in large numbers—the baby boom. Although many Ontarians still tried to keep their food bland, it was a losing battle. Exposure to different cultures through travel and in print, TV and radio precipitated a thirst for new ideas.

Changes in Canadian immigration policies profoundly affected the country's dominant religious and cultural practices, as well as its media portrayals. With this came great changes in the perception of food, including garlic. However, garlic was still meted out in tiny quantities, as if it possessed supernatural powers. Eat too much of it, and Canadians might suffer dire consequences. But changes were afloat, some from surprising quarters, far removed from the world of food.

Religious changes played a big part. This included the Second Vatican Council. From 1961 to 1965, Vatican II attempted to address Catholic doctrine in the modern world. One of its effects was a shift in the use of food from religious symbol, to an ecumenical bridge to reach people from other denominations and religions. This led to Catholics learning about the eating habits and dietary restrictions outside their church. The distinction of food as an object of ethnic, and not religious, interest has had a further effect on the dissemination of culinary habits. Food differences among populations are celebrated, not shunned. As Michael and Ellen Desjardins put it, Canadians are more interested in tasting "local Mennonite food or supporting the Mennonite sale of fair trade coffee, then they are in attending Mennonite religious services."[79]

Amy Morris shared with me her experience of learning about garlic thorough her church. Morris grew up in a fishing village, Bathsheba, in Barbados. She doesn't recall garlic being used by her mother, who was proud of her Little England heritage (Barbados was a British colony until 1966). When she arrived in Canada in 1969, Morris was exposed to many cuisines, and garlic itself, through St. George the Martyr Anglican Church in Toronto. "There were people from all different nationalities at the church, from India, Pakistan, the Caribbean Islands and old Canadians from Newfoundland and Nova Scotia. I got to taste many prepared food dishes. After my mother visited Canada and accompanied me to church, she started to use garlic in her cooking, more than me."[80]

Publishing also influenced Canadians' attitude toward new cuisines. Cookbooks and their authors helped introduce garlic to the hearts and stomach of families in North America. One such book was *Mastering the Art of French Cooking, Volume I*, published in 1961. Its introduction was a watershed moment in cookbook publishing. Its author, Julia Child, and her collaborators, Simone Beck and Louisette Bertholle, brought classic French cooking—and garlic—into Canadian and American homes. They demystified French cooking for the homemakers of the day. Child combined the cookbook with a TV show called *The French Chef*. She became famous for her imperfect French pronunciations and her high-pitched, slightly British-sounding voice. Her practical advice was easy for North Americans to understand: "You make Beef Bourguignon just the way you make any other kind of a stew." It lent her an air of authority but also made her approachable.

Her book received the imprimatur of no less than *New York Times* food critic Craig Claiborne. In his 1961 review, Claiborne lamented that prior to this work, "scores of books have been published in English on the subject of French cuisine. Many of these books have been written by French chefs via the test kitchens of publishing firms with myopic and underfed editors."[81] But in the case of garlic, Child minced her words just a little, in order to appeal to people who had never tried it.

Her guidelines for using garlic indicated that a single "medium clove" of garlic is the equivalent of one-eighth of a teaspoon. That's a very small amount of garlic. (One clove of Ontario Music garlic is about two teaspoons—sixteen times a single clove mentioned in her cookbook!) Perhaps she was playing to her conservative North American audience. Yet on her television show, *The French Chef*, her real sentiment became apparent. In her demonstration for making *boeuf bourguignon*, she can be seen using a clove from a very large bulb of garlic. She used two to three times the amount called for in the recipe and then suggested to "add more garlic" if you choose. In other words, a garlic novice could interpret the directions precisely, but braver cooks were given license to use their own judgment.

Graham Kerr wasn't one to concede to his editor. He told me that a book publisher in the late 1960s requested that he completely remove garlic as an ingredient from a book he was writing. Garlic "would not appeal to audiences in the Midwest," the publisher's rep told Kerr. "Please remove garlic from your recipes." Kerr was horrified. After traveling with his wife, Treena, around the world in search of classic dishes for his TV show, *The Galloping Gourmet*, he had learned that garlic played an integral part in virtually every cuisine. He could not *not* use garlic. So he kept the garlic and gave up the publisher. (He quickly found a new one.)[82]

Two homegrown talents furthered the ascent of garlic in Ontario. One was John Szpin. What motivated him to get into cooking was extreme hunger. His son, Richard Szpin, tells his father's story:

*After subsisting on sawdust and glue for two years in a concentration camp, my father was liberated in 1945, weighing ninety pounds. When the British liberated the camp, they asked each prisoner what they did by profession. My father thought he might get more food by saying his profession was a cook. He was placed in a kitchen as a cook and he just learned as he went along, but I think he may have been a natural because in no time he headed the cooking staff. When a wealthy entrepreneur, steel baron Sir James Dunn, came as part of the Canadian-British contingent to visit the camp, my father was introduced and offered a position as a chef in his hotel in Sault Ste. Marie. In a very short time, he became the head chef at the Windsor Hotel, the biggest hotel in the city…He later became co-owner of the Golden Steer, the most outstanding restaurant in all of the Sault Ste. Marie area in the 1950s and 1960s, and also starred in a TV cooking show on CJIC. With his Polish accent, it probably made the show more authentic, though in that era I could guess there was some bias against new immigrants...As a European, garlic would have been an ingredient used in his cooking daily, but father was very cognizant of the uneducated palates of Canadians, so he eased them into his dishes.*[83]

Another homegrown talent was Etta Sawyer. Sawyer trained in the Noble House of Esterházy in Hungary, where garlic was a staple in the cooking. She appeared annually for about twenty years, starting in 1962, at the Kitchen Theatre at Toronto's Canadian National Exhibition, and went on to run a cooking school. Her daughter-in-law, Laurie Oehy, remembered her liberal use of garlic: "Her students would gasp when they saw her add garlic to a dish. That would be the cue for Etta to add more garlic, just to get a reaction. It was a sign of her showmanship and artistic license."[84]

The 1960s brought youth culture, lunar landings and religious shifts, along with waves of immigrants, all of which would forever change Canada's demographic and culinary landscape. So it made sense that one day in 1967, Executive Chef Georges Chaignet at Toronto's Inn on the Park

Chef Etta Sawyer and a guest at a cooking demonstration, Canadian National Exhibition's Kitchen Theatre, early 1960s. *Courtesy of Records & Archives, Exhibition Place.*

tried something new. Known for his sophisticated French cuisine, Chaignet was genuinely concerned with a particular customer's complaint. As food critic James Chatto described in his book *The Man Who Ate Toronto*, a certain Mrs. Amar Patel was the one having lunch at the Inn on the Park that day. She had come to try the day's special, "From the Chafing Dishes of India," but she was disappointed by their flavours. Those chafing dishes were filled with "the curious travesty of Moghlai cooking that European chefs were trained to prepare: chicken, shrimp, or beef in a sort of béchamel sauce coloured with curry powder." Afterward, Patel "called the manager and gently tried to explain that this was a little less than authentic." So, the chef asked her to prepare him a real Indian dinner. Said the kitchen sous chef, Jacques Marie, after tasting her meal, "She showed us what curry is really about. It was a new world to me."[85]

Soon after, Patel was hired to teach the kitchen staff the principles of Indian cooking, which would have included the essential use of garlic and ginger. By 1970, she had founded the Indian Rice Factory, which became a Toronto institution for more than forty years.

But the changes to Ontario foods were not restricted to "ethnic" cuisine. Take two top Toronto restaurants, Winston's Restaurant and Carman's Dining Club. Throughout the 1960s and '70s, these restaurants emerged at opposite ends of the garlic spectrum. Winston's, named in honour of Winston Churchill and Anglo cuisine, had been reimagined from its original incarnation as a burger joint in 1946. It remained true to its name by serving food within the tight orbit of what it imagined Anglo-Torontonians would like. By 1966, John Arena had come on board as its new owner and manager and kept the tradition going, including a rule banning garlic. Arena said that they never used it, and it's no wonder—it might have upset the powers that be. In his book *The Canadian Establishment*, Peter C. Newman aptly described its lunchtime clientele: "The standard Winston's two-hour lunch is a daily convention of the Establishment's illuminati (not a high-tech microchip carver in the bunch) who want to remain within frequent sight and range of those who make the decisions that count—in other words, one another… They have chosen this restaurant as a stage on which to parade themselves and their egos."[86]

While patrons at Winston's ordered "shrimps wrapped in filet of Dover sole, a specialty of the house," across town, a Greek immigrant took an opposite tack. Arthur Carman, born Athanasios Karamanos, had the impudence to challenge the stereotype of what a great restaurant can be. In 1959, he opened Carman's Dining Club, tucked behind Maple Leaf Gardens. While

Carman's Dining Club owner Arthur Carman, *left*, chats with Prince Philip, Duke of Edinburgh and husband of Queen Elizabeth II. *Courtesy of Carmen's Steakhouse.*

Winston's refined British airs exemplified the hushed diplomacy espoused by its owner, Carman's gloried in garlic.

Clientele at Carman's was an international who's who, including Jimmy Durante, Sammy Davis Jr. and Prince Philip, Duke of Edinburgh. Chris Likourgiotis once bussed a table for Anthony Quinn before being promoted to the kitchen. Likourgiotis recalled the restaurant's distinctive odour, "When I turned onto Alexander Street from Yonge to start my shift at Carman's, I could already smell the garlic." It's no wonder—the kitchen staff was churning out garlic-infused dishes every waking hour. Carman's infamous garlic bread was made with coarse chopped garlic mixed with an equal amount of butter slathered on bread. Imagine the smell after three or four minutes under the broiler?[87] Radio host Ted Woloshyn was a frequent visitor to Carman's. He recalls Arthur proudly telling him, "on more than one occasion the local constabulary had been called to the restaurant to investigate reports in the neighborhood of a slow-moving cloud smelling of garlic."

Back at Winston's, a clove of garlic was as welcome as a spilled martini. Arena recalled that one day in 1988, Executive Chef Frank Staheli served Shrimp with Garlic (see recipe on page 119). The patron turned up his nose and sent it back to the kitchen. Arena continued with his garlic-less menu, relying on savoury herbs like rosemary and thyme for flavour.[88]

Although at opposite ends of the garlic spectrum, the two restaurants often served the same customers. Arena wondered why some of his clients, like Pierre Berton, came to Winston's for lunch but would go to Carman's for dinner. Haberdasher Harry Rosen may have the answer: "Upon arriving home from an evening at Carman's, just as I entered the door, in fact, before both feet were in the door, my wife, who would be in another part of the house, could smell the garlic. 'You've been to Carman's!' she'd call out. From three rooms away." That didn't stop Rosen from being a frequent visitor to Carman's from 1963 to 1975. Perhaps smelling of garlic was part of the ritual—his dry cleaner must have loved him. But no self-respecting captain of industry would dare go to an afternoon meeting reeking of garlic. A 1960s executive could return to work with the sweet smell of gin on his breath. But garlic? No way.

Garlic sometimes prevailed as an object of negative cultural stereotypes at the same time that it was praised. Image from "A Breathtaking Chew," *Ford Times* article on the virtues of cooking with garlic (1971). *Courtesy of Ford Motor Company.*

In restaurants in the 1960s and '70s, certain garlic dishes ruled: escargot, Caesar salad and, of course, garlic bread. For persecuted garlic lovers, these were oases in a bleak culinary landscape. CBC host Stuart McLean recalled that his mother didn't keep garlic in the house because "it smelled up the cutting board." His father loved going to restaurants and would look for the garlic dishes.

Canadian actor Martin Short was once upstaged by garlic itself in the person of Thunder Bay–born musician Paul Shaffer at a theatre in 1970s Hamilton. Short was starring in a controversial drama with a gay storyline, and Shaffer was there in the audience with friends Gilda Radner and Eugene Levy.

Short tells the story in his book, *I Must Say: My Life as a Humble Comedy Legend*. "We planned to go to dinner after the show at a really good high-end restaurant in Hamilton called Shakespeare's. Paul was especially excited about this because I had told him that Shakespeare's had the best garlic bread in Canada. It was all Paul could talk about for days: 'I'm so excited to try the garlic bread! Oh, and of course to see you in the role of Rocky in a fabulous production of *Fortune and Men's Eyes*!'

Shaffer was so fixated on the garlic bread that when he learned, while watching Short's performance, that Shakespeare's was closed that evening, he walked up to the stage and interrupted Short: "Pssst…Marty! Horrible news! Shakespeare's is closed tonight! Wink if Bavarian's makes sense."[89]

Unfortunately, a whole generation of erstwhile garlic eaters was misled by the taste of garlic powder. For true garlic lovers, it was a poorly executed forgery. For some, the addition of garlic, even powdered, made food exotic or "gourmet." Dinah Koo remembered that when she started Dinah's Cupboard, she had to bring dried herbs in bulk from New York. In an interview with a journalist at the time, she was asked, "How can you make a living selling parsley and dried garlic powder."[90] Dinah's Cupboard was a hugely successful business for more than forty years.

## Chapter 6

# HOME INVASION

*Eventually he ripped out all the lilacs, replacing them with garlic.*
—*Josie Emond*

The 1980s brought us a garlic boom that has yet to abate. Garlic entered our consciousness in a tripartite attack: young, pioneering chefs; the spread of "ethnic" cooking; and a growing interest in healthy food.

Until the 1980s, a few high-end restaurant owners in Toronto favoured exotic, imported ingredients like truffles in an attempt to attract Toronto's aspiring middle class and the Bay Street crowd—people looking to demonstrate their sophistication. Things changed when a few chefs broke free from the yoke of the ubiquitous "continental" steakhouse and "French" cuisine.

Across the city, chefs who championed seasonal produce trumpeted their *nouvelle cuisine*. Toronto's culinary identity began to emerge, one emphasizing "new" flavours and locally produced food in its restaurants. It was these chefs—like Greg Couillard, Michael Stadtländer, Jamie Kennedy, David Cohlmeyer and Frank Prevedello—who helped make it acceptable to eat dishes with garlic.

I recall my sister Betsy, an aspiring chef at the time, telling me about an early '80s restaurant opening in downtown Toronto. The owner set up a burner at the front of the restaurant. Over a low flame, he sautéed garlic in fresh butter. The fumes drifted into the street, the better to woo would-be cognoscenti. The place was soon filled with hungry passersby. Garlic was no longer something to be hidden; its smell could now be used to attract diners.

Chefs increasingly cook with Ontario produce, including garlic. *Left to right*: Chef Yuchi Zhang (Gushi Toronto) and Farmer Warren Ham (August's Harvest, Gads Hill, Ontario) at the Toronto Garlic Festival. *Photo by Peter McClusky.*

Farmer, chef and sustainable food expert David Colhmeyer was an early garlic advocate. When he opened his restaurant, Beggar's Banquet, in 1972, the advice from other chefs, including Willy Brand—the renowned instructor/ chef at George Brown College—was unequivocal: don't use garlic. At that time, the Spadina bus, going through Chinatown, was infamous for its garlicky smells. But to Cohlmeyer, "it smelled good." Naturally, he chose to use garlic at his restaurant. Twenty-five years later, still a garlic advocate, he then was working out of his farm, Cookstown Greens. "Garlic greens were the first crop of the year. One day, I was making a delivery of scapes to the Four Seasons Hotel. While I was waiting for the chef, another deliveryman, he was Iranian, said, 'Is that what I think it is? My grandmother is very sick, and that's what she wants. Can you give me some?' I didn't have any extra scapes, but the chef gave some from his order to the fellow."[91]

According to Cohlmeyer, Ontario's locally produced food was featured in the Ontario Pavilion at the 1986 World Exposition Vancouver where

Alice Waters, a champion of California cuisine found inspiration from it. Ironically, the value of farm-to-table meals and locally grown garlic was not well appreciated in Ontario at the time. Ontario farmers received sparse compensation for their efforts to provide fresh produce. Many California farmers, such as Michael Ableman, got their start in Ontario but moved to California, where locally produced food was better appreciated.

Greg Couillard grew up in a Toronto emerging as a multiethnic, multicultural capital. He recognized that all these cultures had one thing in common: garlic. Couillard's first job in a Toronto kitchen was at Troy's, "a chic restaurant, where I made the garlic butter. That flavour drove me crazy. I'd spread it on bread and lick it off my fingers."[92] Seeing what was going on in the city around him and at forward-thinking restaurants like Troy's, Couillard knew that change was in the air, and it smelled like garlic.

While the changes in Toronto's restaurants continued, a quiet revolution was happening. Canadian immigrants (and their descendants) were championing the way Canadians cooked at home. For generations, they had been using fresh ingredients and cooking their incredible food without pretention. Their influence continued, unabated, behind the scenes. It was a battle fought house by house, meal by meal and, in some cases, from garden to garden.

One of these food champions was Anne Sorrenti, a third-generation Canadian of German-Italian ancestry. By the time she was eight years old, she knew her way around a kitchen and had achieved a remarkable level of competence. "I started a lot of fires in the kitchen, but I knew how to put them out." After her parents divorced, Anne and her sister did even more cooking. It was not a big deal to make a grand meal after school, and garlic was always part of the food. She recalled one meal that she cooked as a twelve-year-old girl: bruschetta with raw garlic, tomatoes and olive oil, followed by pasta with garlic and butter. "We used so much garlic, but for us, it was normal. We didn't get just how much garlic we used until afterwards, when we went out to the park to hang out with our friends. I guess we were upwind of them when one of them said, 'Why do you smell like that?' We didn't think we stunk of garlic."[93]

Sorrenti's cooking prowess was not cowed by a bunch of kids in the park, but it opened her eyes. While the Sorrentis had homemade tomato sauce, her friend ate Chef Boyardee. And while the Sorrentis ate *pasta aglio e oglio*, her friend had Stouffer's Chicken Divan (a chicken broccoli casserole) with Minute Rice. And who was the embarrassed one? The family with the homemade tomato sauce or the family with the red, white and green labeled can of Chef Boyardee? Sorrenti explained:

> *My friend Veronique had store-bought canned food in her house, like Chef Boyardee. We couldn't afford canned food. To me, homemade tomato sauce meant we were poor. Boyardee meant not poor. And the novelty of Boyardee, I really liked it when I first tasted it at Veronique's house. Her mother served it with white wonder bread and margarine. It was good tasting as a novelty, but I knew then that it wasn't good food. I wouldn't have classified it as "Italian." The real eye opener was when Veronique came over to my house one day after school and tasted my pasta. I was embarrassed at first, carrying cans of tomato sauce upstairs from the cantina. But she thought it was amazing. She had never tasted anything like it.[94]*

Canned food as a mark of social status had been around for a while. As a young girl in 1930s Beaverton, Ontario, my aunt Nina, like Anne Sorrenti, was envious of kids who ate canned food. She suffered the "indignity" of having to eat fresh, delicious food from her mother's garden. Today, fresh fruits and vegetables are widely accepted, while Chef Boyardee has come down a notch or two on the social ladder.

Seeing Veronique's reaction to her cooking gave Sorrenti a different perspective on the recipes she learned from her Nonna. The encore came when Sorrenti found herself cooking at Veronique's house:

> *Veronique's mother was happy to not be in the kitchen. She was a '60s child; I think domestic life grated on her, and Veronique's British-born father loved my cooking—a beef stew or Pasta Fagioli, simple dishes but delicious. And our home was an open house in the neighbourhood, with kids coming over all the time to eat dinner. We didn't change things up; we cooked the way we cooked for ourselves, including garlic, and they loved it. Now, thirty years later, my son Alexander cooks for his friends after school.*

It was no accident that Sorrenti would develop a passion for cooking. Her grandmother and grandfather ran a Toronto store, Sorrenti's Variety, at College Street and Augusta, from 1960 to the early '80s:

> *They sold cigarettes, ice cream, dolls, Playboy magazines…but what made it special in the neighbourhood was the cooking. Nonna Palmira and Nonno Reginaldo lived upstairs and cooked in the main-floor*

*kitchen, at the back of the store. Customers came from all over, and they would ask my grandmother about the cooking: "Nonna, what are you cooking today? Ragout? It smells so good. I wish my mother could cook like that."*

*Sorrenti's Variety was like the UN, with people coming and going all the time. I would run errands for her. Next door there was a Spanish bar. They made sausage on a bun; it was delicious and garlicky. I'd pick up three to take back to the store. I'd be in a hurry to get back so I could eat mine and would hear the owner behind the bar calling after me, "Tell your Nonna Palmira she's a saint." One day, two dancers came into the store from the flamenco bar three doors down. They were in their costumes, and they had paella for us. It was the first time I tried paella. I could smell the garlic. It's around that time that I discovered Kensington market—or then, in the '80s, it was called the Jewish market. It was different from the rest of the city. People tried each other's food. In the evening, you could smell the cooking and the garlic.*[95]

Sorrenti was spreading the gospel of garlic to the masses. Across Ontario, garlic was entering our lives. In some cases, it was a home invasion. Josie Emond recounted a story her friend told her about an Italian Canadian garlic grower and his Bible-thumping landlady:

*A friend in Collingwood had a neighbour, Mrs. Bosworth, who lived alone on Pine Street and had a backyard full of lilacs. She had a tenant, Tony, who was born in Canada of Italian descent. He drove a taxi for a while, which he gave up. He had lived with two widows for a while, and when they died, he moved in with Mrs. Bosworth. Mrs. Bosworth was a "big C" Christian. The backyards of the houses on Pine Street all backed onto Main Street, so all the houses had huge yards. Mrs. Bosworth's yard was at least sixty feet long. She had two benches among the lilacs and would sit and enjoy their fragrance during cool summer evenings while she sipped her tea.*

*She was a preacher, and with her brother, who was also a preacher, would go on preaching tours in the States, in tents. One year in the fall, Mrs. Bosworth and her brother went on one of their tented preaching tours. It was while they were away that Tony got the idea to plant a few garlic cloves in the garden. There was a little space, unclaimed by the lilacs, in the corner of the yard. What harm could it do? Tony planted a handful of cloves.*

*Mrs. Bosworth didn't notice until the next spring, and a little dismayed, but also a little charmed by Tony's love of garlic, thought nothing of it. What's the harm in a few garlic plants? The following year, he planted a few more cloves, and the next year, more. For a couple of years, the change was so slow she didn't notice. It was like watching an ice cube melt. It occurred to her one evening as she poured her tea. Something was different. The garlic was taking over. Tony was ripping out lilac plants and planting garlic. She complained to a friend, saying, "What can I do?" "You can tell him to stop," was the sensible reply. It was around this time that Tony set up shop on the front porch, selling garlic in two-quart and four-quart baskets. As business picked up, he invested in a little advertising. He tore a piece of sheathing from a Bible crate in the basement. On it he painted the words, "The Garlic Man." It hung by a string from a post on the porch. Business was booming. Eventually he ripped out all the lilacs, replacing them with garlic. But he left the two benches alone.*

Many resisted. For some people, garlic still had an undesirable image. Torontonian Marie Klassen told about one stalwart: her own mother. It would take a health food craze to bring her around. Klassen's mother regarded garlic as something undesirable, something used by a "lower class." If you used garlic, you might become like "them." Marie Klassen explained the attitude of her own mother growing up:

*Garlic was connected to poverty, and even though my mother's family was also poor, they were not immigrant poor—they were poor but proud, poor but educated, poor but Baptist, poor but unaccented English-speaking. There was no way they were going to have fingers that smelled like garlic. Heavily and luxuriously flavoured food was somehow decadent and thereby unchristian, and rather provocative as well. Pleasure was not to be had! Who really knew where garlic could lead?* [96]

Healthy, fresh-cooked food and stir-fries caught her mother's attention. She was particularly interested in cooking with a Chinese wok. But some of the recipes called for garlic, and there lay the dilemma. Garlic was meant for low-class heathens, and powdered garlic would not suffice in this new style of cooking. What could she do? She needed fresh garlic to make her stir-fries delicious. She soon had an epiphany. It wasn't long before Klassen's mother was growing garlic in her garden.

Cooks everywhere were throwing caution to the wind. Physics teacher Barry Gragg recalled the day in the late 1980s when he abandoned his garlicky trepidation. "I lived in a communal house in Toronto. There were lots of students. One night we were making dinner. I thought I was being sophisticated by telling a woman who lived there to rub the salad bowl with a piece of crushed garlic. She didn't miss a beat. She said, 'That's bullshit. Just put it in.'"[97]

Garlic was no longer something to be hidden, disguised or consumed in tiny doses. It was something to be loved, not sneered at. It had come into its own.

*Chapter 7*

# TEAM GARLIC

*In the not-too-distant past, garlic was referred to as being among "other spices." Now garlic is on the marquee.*

—*Suman Roy*

The secret is out. Many people are aware of garlic's attractions, and demand for garlic has never been greater. And when demand soars, the supply side tries to keep up. Beginning in the 1980s, Ontario became a significant grower. But local garlic farmers suffered more than a few bumps and bruises on the way.

A few garlic trailblazers set the stage for Ontario garlic farmers and gardeners to follow. Ted Maczka was a fixture in the Canadian garlic industry and was something of a cult figure at garlic events and festivals (see portrait in color section). Part showman, part funnyman, he was a garlic evangelist. From his farm in Prince Edward County, Ted answered questions for gardeners and farmers across Canada and was regularly featured on radio and in newspapers. Mark Cullen interviewed Ted on his CFRB radio show in 1995. Ted was in Toronto for the Royal Winter Fair, where he started garlic competitions in 1987. "Ted offered me a garlic brownie after the show, but I didn't want to have reeking breath."[98] (See recipe for Black Garlic Brownies on page 134.)

After coming to Canada in 1952 from Poland, Ted trained as a tool and die maker. Although he had always gardened, it wasn't until he heard that Canada imports most of its table garlic from China that he got inspired to

Canadian Garlic Festival, located in Sudbury, Ontario. *Photo by Dennis Harasymchuk.*

start growing it in a larger scale in the 1970s and became a spokesperson for Ontario-grown garlic.

Known also as the "Fish Lake Garlic Man," he sits close to the roots of the Ontario garlic family tree. He inspired many people, including several founders of past and current garlic festivals, myself included. Mary Stefura started the Canadian Garlic Festival in Sudbury in 1991. She invited Maczka to her second annual Canadian Garlic Festival but was nervous at first. "When I called the city clerk in his hometown, asking for Ted's telephone number, they said, 'Oh. Ted. Ah. Okay.' I wondered if I had made a mistake. So, when Ted arrived in Sudbury the night before his appearance at the festival, I asked a friend to meet him for dinner. Well, it turns out that Ted had invited everyone in the restaurant to come to the festival the next day. He was a live wire."[99]

Even his granddaughter, Ally, didn't quite get Maczka's pontifications. Later on, she realized, "It wasn't logical, but his passion for his craft was mesmerizing and what made him so unique."[100]

I was lucky to meet Ted before he passed away on December 30, 2013. I invited him to give a talk at the 2013 Toronto Garlic Festival. Afterward, visitors swarmed him with questions, and as long as he talked about garlic they were happy to listen. It was a cold morning, Ted was feeling a bit chilly, so I gave him my sweater. My last impression of Ted that day was when he stopped talking about garlic just long enough to pull the sweater over his head. His head popped out, he straightened his collar and then continued to talk. He was a talkative man. Wayne Greer, who was a founding member of the Perth Garlic Festival and attended meetings with Ted, said that to keep within schedule, they'd let him talk for as long as he could hold a book at arm's length.[101]

At his memorial, I came to realize that Ted's passion for garlic was a lightning rod for something much bigger. It was while talking with his granddaughter Ally that I understood that Ted believed in the importance of independent thinking and that garlic was a way for him to express this belief. It tore me up to see Ted's garlic hat one last time on display. Ted's Fish Lake Garlic Water remains one of my favorite recipes, and calls for just two ingredients (as told to Jim Dyer): pureed garlic with vodka poured over it.

The most commonly grown garlic in Ontario is known as Music. A strain of Porcelain, it was named after Al Music, who came to Canada in 1956 from Bosnia (in the former Yugoslavia). Al got his first few bulbs from his Polish neighbour, who in turn got some from a farmer. He planted these and noticed that one in particular produced large bulbs with four to five tightly wrapped cloves. These proved to grow very well in Ontario soil, and Al was soon selling and giving away his "Music" garlic far and wide. Today, it's the most popular locally grown garlic in the province. Al is also a co-founder of the Garlic Growers Association of Ontario.

Garlic came to Warren Ham in an innocuous way: in a plate of Rogan Josh at an Indian restaurant in London, Ontario. The garlic and ginger combination—like a pair of evenly matched tennis pros battling it out even as they complement each other—it was a new taste for the young student. He asked the owner how it was made. Later, he came across an article about Ted Maczka. The first taste of garlic and the story about Ted tantalized him. The rest is history. Ham has been growing garlic for thirty years. His August's Harvest garlic can be found in major grocery chains across the province. Ham was instrumental, along with Ron Deichert, in starting the Stratford Garlic Festival.[102]

The Stratford festival is one of several garlic festivals in the province. The festivals feature Ontario farmers showcasing several varieties of garlic, including rare and heirloom types, plus great food and garlic-related products. Their offerings—from film screenings, informative talks and contests to beer and wine, musical performances, braiding workshops and cooking demonstrations—vary from festival to festival.

Wayne Greer first got intrigued while working as a firefighter in Ottawa in the early 1970s. It's probably not a coincidence that Greer's uncle's wife in

Timmins was Polish. She kept a garden and grew garlic. It was on a grocery run for the fire department that he got the garlic bug. He recalled, "One night, I was sent out to get groceries at the local store. I saw the garlic sitting in the produce display, and it struck me: it was imported, Chinese and it was dried up. Back then, you couldn't buy local garlic in the stores, except in Little Italy, on Bell Street—the residents all grew garlic in their yards."

He continued, "A little while later, I bought a ten-quart basket of Ontario garlic from a Mennonite farmer at the market in Kitchener-Waterloo and planted a few cloves. At the firehouse, they looked at you strange if you ate garlic. I did put it into soup secretly, but they liked it. There's a new generation in the fire department now—they're more accepting. Their 'Fire House Spaghetti' calls for six heads of garlic and three hundred meatballs."[103]

Along with the Canadian, Perth and Stratford festivals, Ontario offers a bounty of garlic festivals: Carp Garlic Festival, the planned Eastern Ontario Garlic Festival, Haliburton County Garlic Fest, Newmarket's Garlic Is Great Festival, Niagara Garlic and Herb Festival, Toronto Garlic Festival and the Verona Garlic Festival (see the festival list in the appendix).

For the competitive garlic grower, the Verona Garlic Festival hosts the Eastern Ontario Garlic Awards, now in its nineteenth year. Organized by Paul Pospisil, at the garlic awards growers show off their "garlic with pride and win cash, souvenir ribbons, certificates and bragging rights for growing the best garlic in the region."

Pospisil's reputation as the "Garlic Guru" comes from many years' experience growing more than two hundred types of garlic on his farm, Beaver Pond Estates, in Maberly, Ontario. He tests each type for its adaptability to Canadian growing conditions, including their resistance to pests and disease. His quarterly publication, *Garlic News*, is a recognized authority on garlic. Pospisil conducts his annual Garlic Field Day at his farm for local garlic growers and garlic enthusiasts.

In the 1980s, with high-end restaurants, immigrant families and health-conscious, mainstream consumers all clamoring for more garlic, farmers took heed. The market was shifting. For years, tobacco had always been a reliable, high-value crop in Southern Ontario. But in the decades that followed, government subsidies dried up and were replaced with measures discouraging tobacco crops. The Tobacco Transition Program (TTP) was typical of government plans to move crops away from tobacco. Garlic fit the bill as a good tobacco replacement, luring Ontarians away from smoking while promoting the health benefits that garlic brought—doubly advantageous.

Paul Pospisil presenting David Hahn of Forest Farm, Godfrey, Ontario, with the Woodman Trophy for winning the 2013 Eastern Ontario Garlic Awards Championships at Verona, Ontario. *Courtesy of the* Garlic News *and Craig Bakay.*

Garlic farms sprang up across the province in the east, the southwest and the north. Over just a few years, Ontario garlic production covered as much as four thousand acres (1,600 hectares). Then trouble struck.

In the 1990s, large quantities of Chinese garlic was "dumped" on the Canadian market. According to farmer Warren Ham, the price paid for their imported garlic didn't even cover its shipping costs. It was devastating for growers, causing many Ontario garlic farmers to call it a day. Ontario garlic production plunged by 90 percent, to just four hundred acres. The Garlic Growers Association of Ontario complained to the Canadian Border Services Agency. The result was a tariff that lasted a decade (1997–2007). Still, it's dubious whether these tariffs actually helped the growers. Some say that the garlic was shipped via third-party countries. Boxes arrived in Canada with the word "China" covered up with a fresh "Philippines" sticker. Same box, new label. Food wholesalers merely turned a blind eye. If you ask Ontario Garlic Growers Association president Mark Wales, the trade tariff had a negligible effect.[104] Ontario garlic did bounce back, despite the imports.

Garlic also got a lifeline from Seeds of Diversity. Its mandate is to protect genetic diversity in plant species. It founded the Great Canadian Garlic Collection to protect and foster the best garlic strains suited to Canadian growing conditions.[105] What really helped the local garlic industry was a growing interest in healthy food, not just packaged "health food." This included fresh ingredients, locally grown. The explosive growth of farmers' markets across the province provides clear evidence of the new interest in locally produced food. The number of markets has increased dramatically, with the economic impact in 2008 estimated at $1.9 billion annually.[106] The garlic boom is part of a larger call for locally grown food. It has become a lightning rod for public antipathy to imports from China. Meanwhile, garlic has become more accepted across cultural, ethnic and class lines. However, it's no surprise that there will continue to be people who hold stereotypes about garlic or who may have allergies to garlic, real or imagined. But as one woman explained, it can be a game changer, and in her case, the stereotype was reversed. She told me about a prospective life partner: "I brought him around to the house to meet my family. He met my sister and, just chatting, said, 'I don't like garlic.' She looked at me with pursed lips and eyebrows raised, as much to say, 'Doesn't eat garlic? The relationship is doomed.'"

Today, farmers are growing garlic across the province, consumers are snapping it up at farmers' markets, garlic festivals and in grocery stores and its popularity continues to grow. While imports—principally from China, but also from the United States, Argentina, Mexico and other countries—still arrive, 25 percent of the garlic we buy is locally grown.[107] Indeed, Chef Suman Roy, who had a stint as chef at Campbell's Soup, noted that garlic now gets equal billing with other ingredients on food labels. "In the not too distant past, garlic was referred to as being among 'other spices.' Now garlic is on the marquee."[108]

*Chapter 8*

# THE CHEMISTRY OF GARLIC

*Allicin accounts for much of the smell and taste of garlic*

We're all familiar with garlic's distinctive odour and taste, but where does it come from? Harvard-trained chemist Dr. Eric Block has been studying garlic for more than forty years. His book, *Garlic and Other Alliums: The Lore and the Science*, brings to life the complexity of allium chemistry. Understanding garlic's chemistry makes for good conversation at the dinner table or at the water cooler. And it may just help your cooking, too.

Imagine the parts that make up nitroglycerin. Separately they're inert and stable. But when mixed, they react violently. Something similar occurs in garlic when an invading pest or herbivore gnaws its way into the plant's cell walls. That bite triggers a tripwire that activates the plant's defense mechanism. Two substances stored separately in thousands of cells in the garlic plant are called into action. When the cell walls are breached by the invader, the enzyme alliinase and the compound alliin instantly react to form allicin. That chemical repels the invading pest, which can't stand the odour. Allicin accounts for much of the smell and taste of garlic. While pests are repelled, we humans have adapted it into our cooking and medicine.

The amount of allicin created in preparation for cooking depends on the number of cell walls breached. And that depends on the method used, such as chopping, using a garlic press or other means (see Cooking Tips). Most of the allicin is created in less than a second. However, additional reactions occur over minutes and hours. Each reaction begets a new chemical reaction, with unique corresponding flavours.[109] Because the chemical composition differs among garlic varieties, their individual tastes and odours also vary.

Garlic boiled or roasted whole—where cell walls are not breached—gets its odour and taste from a different set of chemical reactions than what occurs in crushed garlic. In whole garlic, alliinase cannot react with alliin—they're kept separate. The difference in flavour comes from the breakdown of alliin, isoalliin, methiin and related amino acid–derived compounds, plus other non-sulphur compounds.[110]

Contrary to popular belief, chlorophyll is not an effective agent for reducing garlic breath. It may mask the smell, but it won't remove it. A few vegetables are clinically proven to capture the garlicky smell on human breath. These are kiwi, parsley, spinach and basil. Cooked rice, cow's milk and eggs are also effective.[111] Eggplant, basil and white button mushroom extract (*Agaricus bisporus*) have also proven effective.[112] As a general rule, to reduce garlic breath, eat lots of fresh fruit and vegetables and drink lots of water.

Despite the efforts of chemists and botanists such as Dr. Block, garlic still holds many secrets. Even the most sophisticated machine cannot decipher every chemical process in a lowly clove of garlic.

## Chapter 9
# LORE VERSUS SCIENCE

*If you love your daughter, you'll rub garlic on the soles of her feet.*
*—Dido Lysik*

Claims about garlic's medical and therapeutic effects in ancient lore and modern science can fill a book. It can boost the immune system, reduce blood pressure, reduce the chance of heart disease, protect against cellular damage via antioxidants and is effective against Alzheimer's disease and dementia.

Since prehistoric times, people have used garlic to treat physical and mental illnesses. In ancient India, garlic was a commonly used medication. *The Codex Ebers* (1550 BCE), an Egyptian medical guide written on papyrus, prescribed garlic as a treatment for abnormal growths.[113] In Europe, medical practitioners used garlic throughout the Middle Ages. St. Hildegard von Bingen, the Abbess of Rupertsberg and a leading physician in late twelfth-century Germany, wrote that raw garlic is more effective than cooked garlic.[114] Clearly, she understood that garlic—or what we now know as allicin, a chemical it produces—is heat sensitive.

Ancient camel caravaners had the right idea when they preserved meat by drying it with salt, garlic and red peppers, mashed and rubbed in. We know that garlic has proven antimicrobial effects in meat.[115] Brampton garlic farmer Bob Baloch told how his great-grandfather saw one of the last of these caravans in the late 1930s. "They were coming from modern-day India via Tharparker Desert and going to Persia, Iraq and beyond." Baloch's aunt tried making the preserved meat with garlic and salt when he was a child.

He recalled his mother saying that it didn't taste very good. "But if it's your only form of protein when you're crossing the desert, it was acceptable."[116]

Many ancient beliefs about garlic's medicinal benefits continue to be followed in the modern world. A ninth-century doctor in Baghdad used garlic as an effective treatment for ear infection. His cure included eleven cloves of garlic along with lovage, pine oil and Persian verdigris.[117] One thousand years later, an Ontario woman tried a similar cure. The May 1895 *Ontario Medical Review* records a patient's complaint as told by Dr. Murray M'Farlane. She complained "of great pain and giddiness. Upon examination with a speculum, I found the auditory canal of each ear completely blocked by hard pieces of garlic, which had been inserted on the advice of a friend who extolled its virtues in restoring hearing. Mrs. W——had followed this advice and entirely forgotten about the garlic, which began to swell, causing intense agony and dizziness." M'Farlane not only cured her infection but also helped her overcome her habit of using of garlic as a medical treatment. From that time on, "garlic was banished from the medicine chest forever."[118]

Many other ailments have been treated for centuries with garlic, right up to twentieth-century Ontario. During the 1953 polio epidemic, haberdasher Harry Rosen wore garlic cloves—wrapped in cheesecloth and tied with a string—around his neck. Rosen recalled that his mother and Polish grandfather believed it would protect him from infection at school.[119] This was not a new practice. In fact, people have long used garlic as a medical prophylactic, whether worn, carried or hung over a doorway. Doctors in eighteenth-century England carried garlic in their pockets to ward off the odour of disease.[120]

Toronto chef Dinah Koo remembered her parents' remedy for a cold she caught as a young girl. They applied a poultice—made with crushed garlic wrapped in cloth—directly to her chest. Koo said that the remedy was passed down from her great-grandparents in Canton, China. Evidence suggests that this was not a cure dating back just a few generations. In fact, garlic has been used for medicinal purposes in China for at least three thousand years.

Ancient garlic wisdom does not always survive the cultural leap of immigration. People from different cultures erect metaphorical fences between neighbours. Cookie Roscoe recalled as a child her mother ignoring garlic advice from their neighbour, "Dido" Lysik (Dido means "grandfather" in Ukrainian). It was fall, around 1970, Roscoe recalled. "Mum was doing the last of the garden for the year—dusty, hard work that she'd put off, but it was getting too cold and snow was imminent. She sat me in a corner on the ground for only a minute while she tore out the dead tomato and bean plants and threw them on the compost pile. I had a runny nose and was a cranky child, which is what he saw. I think he may have been teasing her about leaving the garden so late before noticing me." And what did Dido Lysik recommend to Cookie's mother? "Rub garlic on the soles of her feet."

Roscoe's mum, her British sensibilities fully intact, replied, "Thank you kindly for the advice. It's nothing that a good night's rest won't set straight." Dido Lysik leaned over the fence, staring down at them like a pharmacist at a dispensary counter. "Take her socks off. Cut a garlic clove in half and rub the halves on the side of her feet." Roscoe's mum was intent on getting her task done and wasn't interested in his advice. But Lysik stepped up the pressure. "If you love your daughter, you'll rub garlic on the soles of her feet."

Dido Lysik was on to something. His sales pitch used the same logic as corporations in selling their products: appeal to consumer insecurities and repeat it over and over. *If you're a good mother and love your child, you'll buy our product.* It seemed to work on young Roscoe. She recalled looking at Lysik's arched brow and then at her mother, wondering, "Hmmm…maybe my mother doesn't love me."

Another persistent belief is the power of garlic is to ward off vampires. Probably the most popular theory of the origin of the vampire is the disease porphyria, a term for several diseases which are all caused by irregularities in the production of heme, a chemical in blood. Some forms of this disease cause sufferers to be sensitive to light and leads to disfigurement of the skin, including erosion of the lips and gums. These factors could have led to the corpse-like, fanged appearance that we associate with vampires and their dislike of sunlight. Interestingly, people who suffer from porphyria also have an intolerance to foods that have a high sulphur content…such as garlic.[121]

Is it the panacea some make it out to be? Some of what we read or hear in the media may not be true. To help understand this better, let's step back and look at the big picture.

There's an unspoken collusion between scientists, mass media and the general public. The academic dictum of "publish or perish" can lead some scientists to publish shoddy work. And scientific journals are increasingly willing to publish material that's not always well researched or that may be compromised in some way. Once published, this dynamic is reinforced by mainstream news editors. They regurgitate dumbed-down versions of these studies for the general public, further clouding their worth. Editors prefer positive stories about a new health benefit to draw readers. People of every age and walk of life are eager to read about and buy into the next new health fad. This effect is compounded by online news sites, where "clickbait" strategies rule. Stories are favoured not for accuracy but to raise a website's search engine ranking and advertising revenue.

How can we make sense of all the claims about garlic? There are a few things to consider.

## RESEARCH METHOD

It's important to understand how the research was conducted. It matters if a garlic study is done *in vitro* (in a test tube) or *in vivo* (in animals or humans). *In vitro* studies are performed in a controlled environment—test tube or petri dish—outside of a living organism. Although convenient and less expensive than experiments conducted on humans or animals, they do not replicate the exact environment of the human body. For example, there are *in vitro* studies that claim that garlic lowers cholesterol. Yet *in vivo* studies conducted do not produce the same result. *In vitro* and *in vivo* studies in humans often differ in their results. Why? One reason is digestion. The human digestive system is very good at breaking down food into the parts required for human survival, but it's not perfect. In garlic, for example, medically beneficial properties we can see *in vitro* do not survive in the harsh environment of the human gastrointestinal tract. They're not able to get to the part of the body to have the benefit that's observed *in vitro*.[122] Nevertheless, newspapers and health journal editors take *in vitro* studies at face value. They gleefully report that garlic *may* be beneficial for a particular human condition or illness. Paying attention whether a study was done *in vivo* versus *in vitro* can help you distinguish fact from theory.

## AMBIGUOUS LANGUAGE

New studies often have their ambiguous results reportedly widely as fact. *Garlic may be beneficial to health…It's reported that garlic may prevent stomach cancer… Garlic has been shown to possibly prevent the common cold…Researchers believe that garlic may prevent flu.* If the language used to describe results seems unsupported or vague, don't take it at face value.

# WHO PAID FOR THE RESEARCH?

More and more research is paid for by corporations that directly benefit from the research result. This can interfere with the principles of scientific objectivity. For example, there have been cases of sponsoring corporations keeping negative results a secret.[123]

Even the best-intentioned research can be confusing. Dr. Jan Huizinga (Department of Medicine, McMaster University) studies the human stomach. He believes it's possible that there may be components of garlic that get through the digestive process intact and can be effective in the human body. He cites studies where the evidence of garlic's effect appeared to be weak. However, deeper analysis of the research results revealed that a subset of the participants actually showed a significant benefit from garlic. But their results were snowed under by the other participants. And then there are small studies in which an effect was shown, but this is critiqued by lack of rigor because too few patients were studied. Huizinga suggests that while the beneficial effects of garlic might not apply to everyone, it might help those with a particular biological makeup.[124]

If you want to take garlic for medicinal purposes but prefer it in a capsule form, freeze-dried garlic is preferable, as it will retain as much as 80 percent of the allicin content. That's according to Chung-Ja C. Jackson, PhD. Dr. Jackson studied garlic at the Guelph Centre for the Functional Food, Laboratory Service, University of Guelph.[125]

Science simply may not fully understand the benefits of garlic. Dr. Block concedes that "medicine is not just about molecules. It's also about the psychology of feeling positive, which stimulate the bio-molecules that help healing and come from following your grandmothers' advice."[126] What do I do when I feel a cold or flu coming on? I reach for the (Ontario) garlic. Whether it cures me or not, it tastes great.

## Chapter 10
# HOW TO GROW GARLIC

*With a little patience and a few bulbs, you can build up a sizable crop.*

Hardneck garlic has thrived for millennia in the northern hemisphere in a wide range of soil conditions and climates. So if I can grow garlic as a wannabe farmer with only a single squash as my first harvest, so can you. With a little patience and a few bulbs, you can build up a sizable crop. The cloves are broken off of the bulb and planted in the fall. The cold of winter, also known as vernalization, prompts the clove to break open after a period of dormancy. The mature plant is harvested the following year, in late July. Here is a thumbnail sketch on growing garlic, good for both a tiny patch with a single clove or a field with up to five hundred plants. Each step, from planting to weeding and harvesting, is done by hand. This is how to do it:

1. Inspect and prepare your soil.
2. Plant cloves in the fall.
3. Mulch for winter.
4. Spring chores.
5. Summer harvest and curing.

# Inspect and Prepare Your Soil

All soil is made up of finely ground rock particles, created over millions of years, plus living and dead organic matter. It is the size of the particles—from the large particles of sand to the very fine ones found in clay—as well as the presence of minerals and organic matter, that characterizes each soil type. Each type presents specific advantages and disadvantages for growing vegetables, including garlic.

Sandy soil is light and crumbly, or friable. This means garlic bulbs can be harvested with minimal effort. But it's also porous, with lots of space between each particle of sand (imagine the space between beach balls). It cannot retain nutrients and moisture as well as other soil types. However, bulbs grown in a sand-organic soil mix are easier to clean at harvest time.

Clay particles tend to cling together (imagine stacked dish plates). This allows the soil to hold on to water molecules and nutrients important for plant growth.[127] But it can be a nightmare in very dry or wet conditions. Too dry, the clay turns to concrete, resulting in damaged bulbs during harvest. Too much moisture, the clay soil poses other problems. The weight of vehicles, even walking, compacts the particles in soil, making it more difficult for water and nutrients to move freely and for plant roots to develop.

Whether the soil is high in clay, silt or sand, the addition of compost (which contains organic matter) will improve the soil condition for growing garlic. Before planting, add two inches (five centimetres) of manure or other composted material, mixed into the soil with a shovel or garden fork (an implement with four tines.) Compost adds nutrients and organisms important to your soil ecosystem. It also retains moisture, especially important for sandy soil. This is a good excuse to start composting your kitchen waste if you're not already. Consider raised beds if the soil is heavy, in order to facilitate drainage.

# Plant Cloves in the Fall

## *Purchase Seed Garlic*

Do not use imported table garlic for planting. Not only will it grow poorly, but you risk the possibility of infecting your garden or farm field with foreign-based diseases. No self-respecting garlic grower wants to be known as the Typhoid Mary of Ontario garlic. Planting garlic from stock produced near your growing

To release cloves, "crack" the bulb by breaking the skin on the bulb. *Courtesy of Toronto Garlic Festival.*

zone will be better acclimated than bulbs ordered from out of province. Garlic bulbs suitable for planting—seed garlic—can be found through mail order, at garlic festivals and in farmers' markets from late July until October.

## "Crack" the Garlic

Each head or bulb of garlic is cracked or opened to release the individual cloves for planting. Each clove, once planted, will grow into a mature garlic plant. To crack a bulb of garlic, hold it in both hands, stem facing up. Pierce the skin with one thumb, using the other thumb to lever the stem back and forth. Once you've removed one clove, the others will easily break off the basal root plate. With a little practice, you'll find the sweet spot on each bulb. It's preferable to crack bulbs as close to the time of planting as possible. Be sure to leave many layers of skin (also known as "wrappers") intact on each clove.

Cracking garlic bulbs may seem at first to be a tedious task, but I learned to enjoy its Zen-like repetition. Sometimes I'll work on another task while cracking the garlic. For example, I'll crack garlic while on a hands free call with the phone company to inquire about their most recent unexplained charge on my bill. While I'm on hold, I can get all the garlic cracked.

## *Plant the Cloves*

Once your bulbs are separated into cloves, they're ready for planting. Plant in the fall, before the first frost. Garlic cloves can vary considerably in length from a quarter inch to an inch or more (0.6 to 2.5 centimetres), so it's recommended to use a planting depth that's relative to the length of the clove. Use a trowel to dig a hole at a depth of three to four times the length of the clove. Place the clove in the hole, pointy end facing up and flat end down, and cover with soil. Soil depth is measured from soil surface to tip of the clove.

In heavy and clay soil, plant at three times the length of the clove. In loose or sandy soil, plant deeper—four times the clove length. Plant each clove six inches (fifteen centimetres) apart. Pat soil firmly. Plant rows at a distance of ten inches (twenty-five centimetres) between rows. Plant in straight rows, as this makes it easier to weed in the spring if using a hoe or mechanical weeder.

A simple way to create straight rows is to tie each end of a string to a stake and align the string in the row intended for planting. Pull the string tight and push the stake at each end into the soil. Once your row is planted move the string and stakes to the next row.

Plant garlic in straight rows to make weeding easier. *Courtesy of Toronto Garlic Festival.*

## Make a Map

If you grow more than one type of garlic, don't forget to mark each section with bamboo poles, wooden stakes or other suitable markers. Since they can be displaced over the winter by wind, animals and heavy rain (or, as one gardener lamented, kids on toboggans), it's recommended to draw a map of your garlic patch, with the length of each section indicated on the map. Keep it in a safe place.

## Bulbils

Bulbils are an inexpensive alternative to planting from bulbs. Bulbils are found in the scape of hardneck garlic. They are tiny, undivided bulbs as small as a grain of rice or as large as a chickpea (see garlic bulbils in pod in color section). They don't carry any known pests or disease (although they may harbour viruses) and are a low-cost way to grow out your garlic crop. To gather bulbils for planting, farmer Paul Pospisil recommends leaving garlic plants in the ground, with scape still attached, for a week or two after your other garlic plants are harvested. Remove the bulbils from the scape and store in a dry place until planting time. If you grow more than one type of garlic, be sure to label your bulbils. They're planted at the same time as garlic cloves, two inches (five centimetres) deep, and may be planted directly into the soil.

Pospisil recommends planting bulbils in containers with sterilized soil or potting mix to protect them from soil-borne disease. Bury the containers in the garden, slightly raised above the surface. Cover with mulch and take care to weed and water the following spring. Harvest the young plants at the same time you harvest your other garlic. In the first two to three years, the plants will produce small "rounds"—small undivided bulbs (no cloves). Replant the rounds each fall. Within two to five years, they'll produce a mature garlic plant with a fully formed and divided bulb. The Purple Stripe variety can produce a mature plant in as soon as one year.

Why plant bulbils in sterilized, disease-free soil? The quick answer is that it buys time. All plants, including garlic, are susceptible to disease and pests in the soil. Some of these organisms can harbour in the plant from year to year, remaining dormant until the right conditions occur for them to grow. Growing bulbils and rounds in sterilized soil helps ensure that the mature garlic plant, once planted into the field or garden, will be disease free. In other words, they are given a head start compared to if they had been planted into soil that potentially contains disease and pests.[128]

## City Growing

Growing garlic in the city presents special challenges. If your garlic is planted in containers, there's the risk of sudden freezing. Garlic farmer Bart Brusse suggests using a container that's at least thirty gallons (approximately one hundred litres) in volume. "A smaller container can also be used if it's insulated from the cold. Keep it inside a garage or cold room in the basement as long as the temperature is below ten degrees Celsius (fifty degrees Fahrenheit). If kept outside (against a wall helps), cover the whole container with a good insulator—bags of leaves, straw or an insulating blanket such as natural coir (made from coconut husks) or even an old blanket." If the container is on the ground, it will receive some latent heat from the ground. If the container is on a balcony or deck, insulate the bottom. Finally, garlic is not afraid of heights, but plants on a high floor in an apartment building or condominium will be exposed to high winds and possibly colder temperatures—a few extra layers of insulation are recommended.

## MULCH FOR WINTER

Cover your planted garlic with mulch, using weed-free straw, leaves or shredded newspaper. Mulch should be twelve to eighteen inches (thirty to forty-five centimetres) deep. Newspaper or leaves, although readily available, may form a thick mat, impeding young garlic plants. To prevent this, check in early spring to see if some layers should be removed. Mulch serves several functions. Although the ground will likely freeze solid during the winter months, mulch lessens the damaging effect of sudden changes in temperature. In the spring and summer, it suppresses weed growth and helps retain moisture in the soil by blocking the sun's rays. Come spring, don't be surprised to find snakes, toads and nesting birds hanging out in your mulch, snacking on insects, including potential garlic pests. These animals are a natural pesticide. As the mulch breaks down over the season, it contributes to the organic content of your soil. A snow cover also serves as mulch, although by spring it will have melted into the soil. Be prepared to do some weeding.

## SPRING CHORES

### *Apply Fertilizer*

If your location gets less than four hours of direct sun per day, work compost or vegetable fertilizer into the soil beside the row in mid to late April, when the plant starts to grow rapidly. Does the soil need water? Here's a simple test. Take a small handful of soil from your garlic patch and shape it into the size of a marble. Squeeze it. If it does not crumble, it has enough moisture. If water squeezes out of the ball, it has too much. For this test, be sure to gather soil from a few inches below the soil surface.

### *Weeding*

A typical acre of topsoil contains millions of weed seeds—they can lie dormant in the soil for decades. The garden hoe—developed 2,000 years ago—is one of the best tools to manage weeds. A quick pass with a hoe agitates the soil surface, disrupting newly sprouted weeds. Check the

A garden hoe easily removes weeds when they are just three to four inches high. *Courtesy of Toronto Garlic Festival.*

weather forecast before weeding—it's recommended to weed prior to a dry period, when the sun and heat will ensure that uprooted weeds shrivel up.

## Scaping

Hardneck varieties produce a scape (see hardneck garlic scape in color section). If the scape is left on the plant, bulb size may decrease because energy is diverted to bulbil production. Remove the scapes by breaking or cutting them immediately after they've curled and before they straighten out.

# SUMMER HARVEST AND CURING

The harvest is when the mature plant is dug up from the soil. Garlic should be harvested when the tip of three to five of the leaf sheaths have turned brown. It means the plant has reached its maturity and is starting to decay. Why do the leaves provide a clue when to harvest? Each leaf is part of a structure that serves different functions, from photosynthesis to structural support for the stem, to providing a protective layer for the bulb. Because the leaf sheath and covering on the bulb are part of the same structure, the change in colour is an indicator that the plant has reached peak maturity. Leaving the plant in the soil beyond this point will cause the layers on the bulb to decay. It's important to preserve as many of these layers as possible—they protect the bulb during curing and storage. Some farmers advise digging up and examining a few test plants before the leaves have started to turn brown, especially in wet weather. Moist soil can cause the layers on the bulb to degrade prematurely. If this is the case, don't wait for the leaf tips to turn brown. It's time to harvest.

## How to Harvest

Loosen the soil with a fork, spade or other digging tool, taking care to dig straight down—parallel to the stem of the plant, six to eight inches (fifteen to twenty centimetres) deep and at a distance of three to four inches (eight to ten centimetres) from the stem—far enough not to damage the bulb. Lever

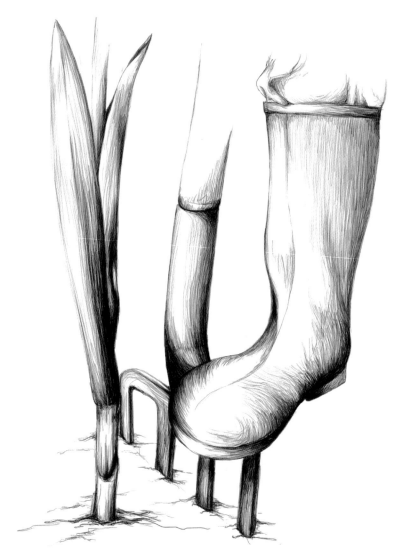

To harvest, use a garden fork, spade or trowel to loosen each bulb. *Courtesy of Toronto Garlic Festival.*

the tool back and forth, gently loosening the soil around the bulb. Now, grasp the base of the plant, near to the soil surface. Pull straight up, taking care to not bend the stem, and gently brush off loose dirt and dead leaves, as these can potentially harbour moisture-loving pests and disease during curing and storage. Lay each bulb on the ground. Before digging up too many plants, check your already harvested bulbs to ensure they have not been damaged by your digging implement. If necessary, adjust your digging method with the next plants to be harvested and send those damaged bulbs to the kitchen!

## Tie the Plants for Curing

Tie garlic plants together in bundles of five or ten (or of your choosing), with a string approximately four feet long—two bundles per length of string. Wrap each bundle twice around using a wide-diameter string, such as hemp rope, to lessen the possibility of cutting into the stem of the plant. Tie tightly to avoid having plants slip out of their bundle—the stems will shrink as they dry. Each set of two bundles is hung by the string to dry or "cure."

Remember, a cut or bruise in the stem or in the leaf sheaths that cover the bulb can allow fungus, mould or other undesirable organisms into the plant.

## Curing

Immediately after harvest, garlic is hung to cure for two to three weeks. This allows moisture to escape and prepares the plant for long-term storage. Hang garlic bundles in a shaded, ventilated locale. In places with high humidity, set up a fan.

## Cut the Bulbs from the Stem

After curing, use household scissors to trim the roots and gardening cutters to cleanly cut the bulb from the stem. Most growers cut the stem very close to the bulb, in part because any amount of stem left behind can pierce adjacent bulbs while in storage. For bulbs that have tight-clinging skins and are difficult to crack, such as the Music strain (a porcelain variety), farmer Patrick Carter prefers to leave about two inches (five centimetres) of the stem on the bulb, as this makes it easier to crack the bulb in preparation for planting.[129]

## Storage

Table garlic (for eating) stores best in a cold room or cellar, or in a clay garlic keeper. Avoid storing in higher humidity, or in temperature extremes, such as near a stove or sunlit window sill. Table garlic stored at room temperature may dehydrate faster. *Do not refrigerate garlic!*

Depending on the variety and strain, garlic can be stored for up to one year. The variation is due to inherent factors in each type of garlic, such as the tightness of the skin on the bulb. No matter the variety of garlic you grow, how you handle the plant during growing, harvest, bundling, curing and storage affects how well the bulbs will store. Since the leaf sheaths covering the bulb serve a purpose similar to human skin—protecting the bulb from potentially damaging organisms—you should ensure that as many sheaths as possible remain on the bulb after harvest. Bulbs with tight-clinging leaf sheaths will likely store the longest. Bulbs with exposed areas on their surface should be the first to be eaten (table garlic) or planted in the fall.

## Pest and Disease Prevention

Fortunately, mammals are not especially interested in garlic, but they can be an indirect nuisance. Squirrels will dig in the soil, looking to bury acorns, and in the process may uproot garlic. The real threat to garlic is smaller and more menacing. Insects and diseases present a serious and often hidden threat. Beware of penicillium mould, bulb and stem nematode, white rot, fusarium, basal plate rot, aster yellows and the leek moth. None of these will make it to the eleven o'clock news, but they are a garlic farmer's worst nightmare. Each manifests in a different way and at different times in the garlic lifecycle.

Penicillium mould causes garlic to decay during storage. When infected bulbs are cracked for planting, airborne mould spores can infect healthy cloves, with potentially damaging results.

Bulb and stem nematode is a microscopic parasite that enters through the root plate or wounds in the bulb. It can lie dormant in the plant until the right conditions arise—it travels well in wet conditions, when it moves from plant to plant, including on a hapless gardener's boot.

The leek moth is an insect pest that lays its eggs on the leaves of garlic. Once hatched, the larvae tunnel into the plant's leaves, leaving it susceptible to bacterial or fungal diseases.

Here are a few common-sense practices as the first line of defense against such threats. Conduct regular inspections during the growing season, culling weak and stunted-looking plants and disposing plant material well away from the field or garden. Practice crop rotation, allowing three to five years between planting of any allium species or plants that are susceptible to the same pests and diseases as garlic. Avoid walking in your garden or garlic field in wet conditions, as your boots (or garden equipment) can transfer water-loving pests from one area of the field to another.

## More Information

Ask your seed source or consult a crop specialist with the Ontario Ministry of Agriculture, Food and Rural Affairs (OMAFRA) on how to manage pests. Know the source of the garlic seed you are purchasing. Some farmers (such as Warren Ham of August's Harvest) plant some of their crop every year with seed virtually free of disease and viruses. This "clean seed" was developed by the University of Guelph with support from OMAFRA and is available to members of the Garlic Growers Association of Ontario (GGAO).

The GGAO promotes awareness and understanding of growing garlic in Ontario. For a nominal annual membership fee, the association runs meetings and field days two to three times per year. Members benefit from timely talks given by scientists from the OMAFRA and have the opportunity to learn from other farmers. You don't have to be a grower to join the GGAO. They're always welcoming new members. They'll accept just about anyone. They accepted me.

Garlic festivals, held annually from August to September across the province, provide information on growing garlic. And you'll find a friendly and informative farmer with tips on growing garlic at any of the hundreds of farmers' markets across Ontario, from Kenora to Kingston (see the appendix for a list of farmers' market).

A good source of information on growing garlic is the *Garlic News*. Editor and garlic guru Paul Pospisil publishes four issues per year from his garlic farm in Maberly, Ontario.

*Chapter 11*

# IN THE KITCHEN WITH GARLIC

*Once in a while, a clove would jettison from my cutting board…we never got those cloves back.*

—*Graham Kerr*

Hidden in every clove of garlic is an abundance of unmatched flavours. But more garlic does not mean more flavour. To coax garlic's flavours and intensity, you need to prepare it properly, though there is no single correct cooking method. It depends on the dish you're cooking. Julia Child's mashed potato recipe calls for thirty cloves, boiled whole, to give it a mellow garlic flavour. Just a single clove, properly pressed or minced, will add an intense taste to a Caesar salad. The difference is in the preparation. This chapter shows how and when to prep garlic to bring out the desired taste and intensity.

## PREP METHODS

Prepping garlic is the first step in cooking with garlic. Most recipes call for the clove to be removed or "cracked" (see page 79) from the garlic bulb. Set aside unused cloves with skin intact for later use.

## Removing the Skin

Some cooks find peeling small cloves tedious and time-consuming. Farmer Ed Burt has been farming on Manitoulin Island since 1950, when he first put his hands in the soil as a very young boy. His grandfather, who taught him, started farming on the island in the late nineteenth century. Here's Bart's opinion on small cloves: "I'm grateful for the opportunity to own a bulb of garlic, to hold a part of creation. I can't imagine being upset about peeling a little bit of skin on a clove of garlic."[130]

### "Side of Knife" Method
Place the cloves on a chopping board and crush them with the side of a cooking knife. This loosens the skin, making it easy to peel away and dispose. Or use a heavy-bottomed jar or cooking pot to whack them on the cutting board. This is the most popular method.

Garlic farmer and baker Heather MacMillan (Little Trickle Farm, Douglas, Ontario) peels garlic. *Photo by Kylah Dobson.*

Graham Kerr, host of *The Galloping Gourmet* television show from 1969 to 1971, mastered the technique of peeling and crushing garlic after an awkward moment on his show. His wife, Treena, told him to be sure to look up at the live audience, not down at his cutting board, when preparing his food on camera. This prep work included peeling garlic cloves. It was there that he came up with the idea of quickly smashing the garlic under the side of his chef's knife, which he would pound with a closed fist while looking at the audience. He told me it took some time to get the technique right. "Once in a while, a clove would jettison from my cutting board into the lap of one of the members of the audience, who were mostly women. We never got those cloves back."[131]

### CUT THE BASE
Cut off the root end of the clove before crushing; this dislodges the skin from the clove's basal plate (root).

### TWO-BOWL METHOD
Place the cloves in a large aluminum bowl, with a same-size bowl (or pot lid) on top. Hold them tightly together and shake vigorously for thirty seconds to loosen the skins. This works best for cloves with loose skin.

### SOAKING METHOD
Soak the cloves for an hour in lukewarm water. Then drain the water and remove the peels.

### PRE-PEELED GARLIC
Some people think that peeling and cutting garlic is too messy and makes their fingers smell of garlic. Personally, I like it—garlicky fingers are my calling card. It helps me meet new friends and is a conversation-starter. For those who prefer it, pre-peeled Ontario garlic is available from The Garlic Box in many supermarkets, in the frozen food section.

## Release the Garlic Flavour

Each method produces a different texture, flavour and intensity. Feel free to experiment. Here, in order of strength, are the most popular methods of releasing garlic's flavours.

### BOILING GARLIC
Boil unpeeled cloves as directed in a recipe. This releases some mild garlic flavours (very little allicin is created), and some say, a subtle sweetness.

### COARSE CHOPPED GARLIC
Peel, smash and chop coarsely. This produces a small amount of allicin. It works best for garlic bits fried in oil. The browned nuggets are a tasty garnish on soup or salad. Coarsely chopped pieces retain some of the clove's structure, leaving most cells intact until the dish is served. As the bits are chewed, allicin is released inside the mouth.

### Finely Chopped Garlic
Finely chopped garlic is stronger and works better in liquids than fried in oil.

### Mortar and Pestle
Peel, place in mortar and grind to a paste. This produces a larger amount of allicin, similar to mincing. The paste it produces works well in liquids and makes a good spread (see Roasted Beets with Almond-Potato Skordalia, page 114).

### Knife-Blade Puréeing
Peel, smash, mince and smash again. This produces the most allicin of any knife-prep method. It works best in liquids.

### Garlic Press
Peel, place in press and squeeze over small bowl. This produces more allicin than any knife-based method and protects your fingers from touching the garlic. Most presses these days are self-cleaning: tiny nubs are aligned to poke out the garlic pulp after use. Scrape off any pressed garlic and add to the bowl. Pressed garlic works best in liquids.

### Microplane
Peel, hold clove in two fingers and grate. This method releases the most allicin and provides maximum garlic flavour. Microplaned garlic works best in liquids. Take care to protect your fingers!

## Timing

Whatever prep method you use, timing is critical. Once the cells of the clove have been breached, add garlic to the recipe as soon as possible. Unlike most ingredients, the volatile compounds that make up the odour and taste of garlic will quickly dissipate. Dr. Chung-Ja Jackson has studied garlic at the University of Guelph and noted that most of the allicin is created within a few minutes. That's why Chef Michael Stadtländer uses garlic immediately after chopping. "I don't like it sitting around when I'm cooking *a la minute*."[132]

## COOKING METHODS

The cooking method used—including duration and temperature— is crucial. It contributes to the variety of flavours released, its level of sweetness, caramelization and the garlic intensity, or heat, of the dish.

### Don't Burn Garlic

Because garlic has less water than onions, it burns easily. I used to brown garlic alongside onions, always wondering where the acrid smell came from. Perhaps I was influenced by a Martin Scorsese film. *Goodfellas* is about the Lucchese crime family, as narrated by Henry Hill (played by Ray Liotta). Henry tells how another family member made pasta sauce in prison. Paulie "had this wonderful system for doing the garlic. He used a razor, and he used to slice it so thin that it used to liquefy in the pan with just a little oil. It was a very good system."[133] Of course, it's not good for one's health to contradict a Mafioso, but I learned that Paulie's method has its risks. Garlic cut with a razor may liquefy in the pan, but it also burns easily. In a few seconds, its smell turns from pleasant to harsh. But how can you avoid burning garlic when making a sauce?

Chef Peter Minaki recommended a simple solution. The moment you can smell the garlic cooking, add the tomatoes. Safer still is adding the garlic *after* the liquid ingredients.

In the right hands, garlic taken to the precipice of being burned does have its place. Chef Curt Hospidales remembered growing up poor in Trinidad, when there wasn't always fish or meat for the pot. "We used garlic to replace the fish or meat flavour. The method was to almost burn the garlic." The resulting flavour is like a reduced beef stock. "Garlic cooked this way was the meat in the pot," recalled Hospidales.[134] (see Provision Rosetta Style on page 129).

### Acid-Based Foods

Vinegar, citrus fruits, tomatoes and other acid-based foods mute garlic's ability to make allicin. Wait ten seconds after releasing the allicin before you add it to an acidic liquid. For example, when adding garlic to a vinegar-based salad dressing or to a pot of tomatoes, wait ten seconds before adding crushed garlic to the liquid.

## Delay Adding Garlic

Add garlic at the end of cooking. Since heat destroys allicin some chefs and home cooks add extra garlic at the end of the cooking process, after the heat is turned off. If your objective is an extra-garlicky taste (or to fight a cold or flu), then you'll want to follow this method.

# OTHER METHODS

Aside from raw and whole garlic, there are other ways to prepare garlic. Methods that involve processing the garlic include black garlic and smoked garlic.

## Black Garlic

Black garlic, otherwise known as fermented garlic, is a black, tar-like substance. Its flavour is a little bit bitter and a little bit sweet, with hints of balsamic vinegar, molasses, licorice and tamarind. Its umami works well in seaweed-based broths, and in desserts it's extraordinary. Despite the name, the process that makes black garlic black is not fermentation (microbial metabolism). Instead, it is due to the enzymatic breakdown of allinase and the Maillard reaction. The Maillard reaction is the chemical reaction that gives a uniquely delicious flavour to browned foods, such as roasted coffee, maple sugar, chocolate and the darkened crust of bread. The reaction results in hundreds of different flavour compounds, depending on the type of food. The flavour of fermented garlic is similar to but distinct from other foods that have gone through the Maillard reaction.

When searching for a pastry chef who could add black garlic to chocolate, I discovered Laura Slack Chocolate Artist. I gained about five pounds as I ate my way into Slack's company. It was worth the weight. Slack made a small batch of the Lestat Truffle—a dark chocolate skull filled with black garlic–infused salted caramel—at the Second Annual Toronto Garlic Festival. It sold out in two hours. Toronto Life included it as one of "50 Crazy Good Things to Eat and Drink" (2013).

Other black garlic delicacies featured at the Festival include Black Garlic Vietnamese Coffee Ice Cream, Black Garlic and Tanzanian Dark Chocolate Truffles, Black Garlic Butter Tarts (see recipe, page 135) and Black Garlic Brownies (see recipe, page 134).

## Smoked Garlic

What started as a method to preserve garlic is now another way to experience a delicious garlic flavour. Bart Nagel at Bulbs of Fire Garlic smokes his garlic using a semi-hot smoke method. One of his favorite recipes is Oven-Roasted Squash with Smoked Garlic and Maple Syrup (see page 113).

Farmer Bart Nagel at Bulbs of Fire grows more than thirty-five types of garlic and smokes garlic using a semi-hot smoke method. *Courtesy of Bart Nagel.*

# DESSERTS

One of the joys in my life is to get friends and strangers to try garlic as a dessert item. Without fail, their reaction is a combination of fascination and delight. *How is it possible that garlic tastes good as a sweet?* Well, the very fact that people have to ask this question (and still don't believe the answer until they taste it) is further proof that garlic has been stereotyped. Consider that twenty years ago, most North Americans considered raw fish with vinagered rice wrapped in seaweed as something far too exotic (or disgusting) to eat. Today, there are sushi shops on every corner. Perhaps garlic desserts will be the next sushi.

The most common step in prepping garlic for a dessert is to roast it (see Roasted Garlic recipe, page 115). Roasting caramelizes the sugar and produces a mellow version of garlic flavour; it does not produce the strong allicin flavour we associate with garlic. Once roasted, the garlic will have a nutty, almost caramel flavour. Its smell and taste is reminiscent of chocolate. At the Toronto Garlic Festival, we've featured Dark Chocolate and Roast Garlic Ice Cream (see page 138) and Salted Caramel Roasted Garlic Infused Truffles. Later, we ventured farther afield, with sweet garlic desserts like Roasted Garlic Butter Tarts (see page 137). Be sure to roast them until the cloves turn dark brown. Which variety has the highest sugar? For home-based cooks, almost any Ontario-grown garlic will serve your purpose, since they have a higher Brix (sugar) content than imported garlic. Feel free to experiment with different types of garlic.

During World War II, roasted garlic with chocolate was created to provide tactical camouflage. Charles Fraser-Smith was a gadget inventor at the British spy agency and is widely credited as the inspiration for the character "Q" in Ian Fleming's James Bond novels. Fraser-Smith created garlic chocolates, to be eaten by British agents parachuting into occupied France. They would smell "Gaelic" to blend into the population and avoid detection by enemy troops. The recipe: Roast whole peeled garlic cloves sprinkled with oil, covered in oven until golden brown. Allow to cool. Dip in melted chocolate and cool on parchment paper. Eat and blend into the crowd.

## GARLIC TASTING

First-time garlic taste testers are often astonished by the variety of flavours, sweetness and heat levels found in Ontario garlic. A very basic taste test is to try fresh, raw garlic on bread or plain crackers. For each type of garlic, use the same prep method, whether it's chopped, pressed or minced. To taste for sweetness, roast whole bulbs or individual cloves, sealed in aluminum foil until well caramelized (should be a golden brown colour, which is the sugars in the garlic caramelizing). Cook for thirty to forty-five minutes at 400 degrees Fahrenheit. Spread on bread or plain cracker.

Emily Leonard selling Garlic Scape Chimichurri off her Casero Taco Bus, Sauble Beach, Ontario. *Photo by Philly Markowitz.*

Ontario garlic bulb. *Photo by Peter McClusky.*

*Above*: Farmers J.P. Gural and So Young on their farm, Samsara Fields, in Waterford, Ontario. *Courtesy of Samsara Fields.*

*Left*: A young visitor at the Toronto Garlic Festival. *Photo by Kate Hamilton.*

*Above*: Harvesting garlic. *Photo by Peter McClusky.*

*Right*: Ontario hardneck garlic scape. *Photo by Peter McClusky.*

Life portrait of Ted Maczka, the "Garlic Man," by Igor Babailov, Hon. RAA.

*Opposite, top*: Apprentice farmer Courtney Dutchak selling Ontario garlic at the Wychwood winter farmers' market. *Photo by Peter McClusky.*

*Opposite, bottom*: Freshly harvested Metechi garlic (Marbled Purple Stripe) laid in field. *Photo by Peter McClusky.*

*Above*: Urban farmer Erica Lemieux hanging garlic to cure. *Courtesy of Erica Lemieux.*

*Left*: Maturing Ontario hardneck garlic plant. *Photo by Peter McClusky.*

*Opposite, top*: Garlic bulbils in pod. *Photo by Peter McClusky.*

*Opposite, bottom*: Ontario garlic bulb. *Photo by Peter McClusky.*

Head (bulb) of Metechi garlic. *Photo by Peter McClusky.*

Chef Anne Sorrenti's garlic veggie stir fry cooking demonstration at the Toronto Garlic Festival. *Photo by Chris Seagram.*

Garlic French Toast with Fruit Compote and Crème Fraîche by Magic Oven at the Toronto Garlic Festival. *Photo by Chris Seagram.*

Roasted Garlic Almond Brittle Coated Apples, served by Roots of Health at the Toronto Garlic Festival. *Photo by Chris Seagram.*

Chef Pawel Grezlikowski's (Hogtown Charcuterie) Honey Garlic Ribs, served at the Toronto Garlic Festival. *Photo by Peter McClusky.*

Bryan "Garlic Man" Mailey's Garlic Braiding Workshop at the Toronto Garlic Festival. *Photo by Chris Seagram.*

Fine art and fine Ontario garlic on display by Sheri and Dianne Fleishauer, Golden Acres Farm, Gads Hill, Ontario. *Courtesy of Toronto Garlic Festival.*

Chef Giacomo Pasquini's (Vertical Restaurant) Homemade Garlic Ciabatta Bruschettone, with a traditional Porchetta with "agliata" (garlic confit and parsley), served at the Toronto Garlic Festival. *Photo by Chris Seagram.*

*Left*: "To Make Paco-Lilla, or Indian Pickle, the Same the Mangoes Come Ever In," re-created by Historic Fort York from a 1747 recipe. *Photo by Melissa Beynon.*

Recently sprouted Ontario garlic clove. *Photo by Peter McClusky.*

*Opposite, bottom*: John Arena, owner of Winston's restaurant from 1966 to 1989, tying garlic stalks. *Courtesy of John Arena.*

*Left*: Two Ontario garlic bulbs. *Photo by Peter McClusky.*

*Below*: Argentino del Piero in his half-century garlic patch. *Left to right*: son-in-law, Peter Mitchell, and grandsons Jordan Mitchell, Scott Mitchell and Mark Mitchell. *Photo by Peter McClusky.*

*Right*: Carrying harvested garlic off the field. *Photo by Ludwig Morris.*

*Below*: *The Order of Good Cheer*, by C.W. Jeffreys. *Library and Archives Canada.*

*Above*: The Ontario Science Centre officiates the Garlic Breath Contest at the Toronto Garlic Festival. *Photo by Peter McClusky.*

*Left*: A young visitor dwarfed by a long garlic braid as Farmer Al Cowan looks on at the 2006 Canadian Garlic Festival, Sudbury, Ontario. *Photo by Alan G. Luke.*

*Chapter 12*

# GOOD GARLIC GROWS IN ONTARIO

*Adding a clove of Ontario-grown garlic to a meal costs only twenty cents.*

Farmers, gardeners and chefs report a wide range of flavours, heat and duration in different strains of garlic. This can be attributed to its *terroir*. Vintners use this term to describe how weather, season, soil type, slope of a field and myriad other factors affect their grapes. The same goes for Ontario garlic.

Ontario farmers grow mostly hardneck varieties (*Allium sativum* var. ophioscorodon). Varieties including purple stripe, marbled purple stripe, glazed purple stripe, rocambole and porcelain deliver flavour variations—everything from mild to very hot flavours. Within each variety there are dozens, if not hundreds, of strains.

Some people say that local garlic is too expensive. But is it really? Adding a clove of Ontario-grown garlic to a meal only costs about twenty cents, and your friends and family will appreciate the difference in flavour. Can you afford that twenty cent investment in your nearby garlic farmer? Or would you rather support a farm factory thousands of miles away that's growing garlic for a uniform shape and size, good only for shipping?

I also hear people complain that it's hard to find Ontario garlic. There's an online garlic map showing hundreds of locations to buy Ontario-grown garlic, including scapes in spring and fresh frozen Ontario garlic

Farmer Bob Romaniuk (Brant County Garlic Company, Scotland, Ontario) with his home-built garlic cracking machine. *Photo by Peter McClusky.*

*Opposite, top*: Planting garlic by hand at Golden Acres Farm, Gads Hill, Ontario. *Photo by Peter McClusky.*

*Opposite, bottom*: Farmers Bob and Irene Romaniuk (Brant County Garlic Company, Scotland, Ontario) on their homemade garlic-planting machine. *Photo by Peter McClusky.*

in late winter. Search "Ontario garlic map" in your internet browser. Locations are province-wide and include farmers' markets, garlic festivals and grocery stores.

Remember, there's plenty of garlic after the July harvest—supply tapers off by mid-winter. If Ontarians demand more local garlic, the supply will follow. Ask for it at your local farmers' market or grocery store produce section. Store managers will get the message, and farmers will plant more of it.

When buying garlic, make sure that the product label indicates that the garlic is grown in Ontario (or Canada), especially when buying loose garlic. Buying garlic with the label "processed in Canada" does not necessarily mean that the ingredients are from Canada. Read the fine print.[135]

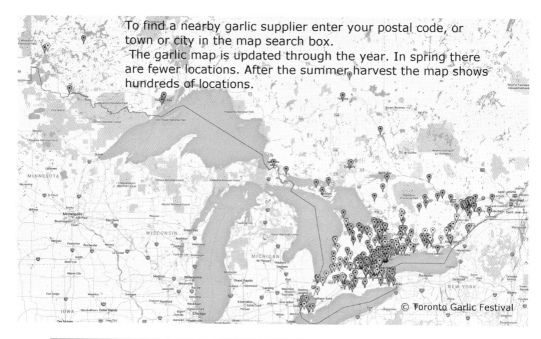

To find a nearby garlic supplier enter your postal code, or town or city in the map search box.
The garlic map is updated through the year. In spring there are fewer locations. After the summer harvest the map shows hundreds of locations.

© Toronto Garlic Festival

*Above*: The Toronto Garlic Festival introduced the "Garlic Map" to show where to buy Ontario-grown garlic. *Map sponsored by Carrot Cache.*

*Left*: Gardens Coordinator Ashrafi Ahmed planting garlic at Regent Park Community Food Centre, Toronto. *Photo by Peter McClusky.*

Ontario garlic scapes growing in front of Collège Français on Carlton Street, Toronto. *Photo by Peter McClusky.*

Farmer Simon de Boer in his garlic field at Langside Farms Organic Garlic, Teeswater, Ontario.

Garlic does not have to be bought "fresh" every week to get the best flavour. In fact, like wine, long-stored garlic can taste better than garlic that's been recently harvested. So stock up on garlic at a farmers' market or garlic festival. Better yet, grow your own. Many community gardens, schoolyards, balconies, backyards and rooftop gardens already feature Ontario garlic.

What to do when the garlic runs out? In my home, we cry ourselves to sleep for a few nights and then we just live with it. We have a few jars of garlic relish and pickled garlic from a local farmers' market. Starting in April or May, young garlic greens are available. They provide a less pungent garlic flavour, but they can be used in salads, soups and dips, like green onions. Scapes are available in June, and then begins the countdown to the July bounty—another harvest and another Ontario garlic festival. You've got plenty to choose from.

# RECIPES

As recipes evolve, so does their use of garlic. Currently, garlic appears in more recipes and with less trepidation. Take *The Joy of Cooking*. John Becker, great-grandson of Irma Rombauer (the original writer), suggested that I look at three recipes: Creamed Mushroom, Pimento Cheese and Spanish Rice. They appear in both the 1931 and the 2006 editions. The differences are striking. The 1931 edition only lists garlic as an ingredient in one of these recipes, Spanish Rice, which advises, "a clove of garlic may be cooked with the rice." By 2006, all three included at least a clove of minced garlic.[136]

The 1963 edition of *Joy* calls garlic "perhaps the most controversial addition to food…as our guests have sometimes been obviously relishing and unawarely eating food with garlic in it—while inveighing loudly against it.[137] Clearly, over the course of its publishing history, the authors have drastically changed their attitudes toward the use of garlic.

I compiled the following recipes to showcase the versatility and flavour of cooking with Ontario garlic. From simple, traditional recipes to more adventurous and sweet garlic desserts, I hope they inspire you to take risks and experiment with garlic's different flavours. I have also included historical recipes to let you try garlic the way it was eaten hundreds of years ago. Some recipes may refer to either a "bulb" or "head" of garlic. Thank you to the local chefs, restaurant owners and farmers for sharing their favourite dishes.

## Soups

# Ajo Blanco with Pinot Noir Grapes and Sunflower Oil

*Chef Jamie Kennedy, Jamie Kennedy Kitchens*

Yield: 6 servings

*8½ ounces (250 grams) whole almonds, unpeeled*
*3 slices white bread with crusts removed*
*1¾ cups (400 millilitres) water*
*5 tablespoons (75 millilitres) apple cider vinegar*
*3 garlic cloves, thinly sliced*
*6 tablespoons (90 millilitres) cold pressed sunflower oil*
*salt to taste*
*1 bunch fresh Pinot Noir grapes*
*¼ cup (60 millilitres) cold pressed sunflower oil*
*approximately 24 small bread croutons*

Bring a large saucepan of water to boil. Add the almonds all at once and bring back up to boil for 3 minutes. Remove almonds with a slotted spoon, and when they are cool enough to handle, pop the skins off. Discard skins and water. Cut the bread into rough pieces and place in a stainless steel bowl. Add water and vinegar and soak for 10 minutes Add water and bread mixture to blender. Begin blending. Add garlic slices and continue to blend. Add blanched almonds and continue to blend. Slowly add sunflower oil and salt to taste. Transfer soup to a pitcher and refrigerate for 2 hours.

Slice grapes in half. A half hour before you are ready to serve your guests, place 6 soup bowls into fridge or freezer. When you are ready to serve, remove bowls and place on table. Pour chilled soup into bowls. Carefully place 3 grape halves on the surface of the soup. Drizzle some sunflower oil on the surface. Use 2 to 3 croutons per portion. Serve.

# RECIPES

## Brazilian Black Bean Soup

*Chef Mario Cassini, Food Consultant, Restaurateur*

*This soup brings me back to my childhood and the memory of watching my aunt Maria cook. She would make this soup and have me stand on a stool to watch the beans being pureed in the blender. The aroma, especially of the garlic, was incredibly rich. It was something very special. Garlic is used in many Brazilian dishes, especially in the southeast of Brazil, where I come from (Belo Horizonte, Minas Gerais). Walking through the streets between 10:30 a.m. and 11:30 a.m., you can smell the aroma of garlic and onions being sautéed as lunch is being prepared on a daily basis.*

Yield: 6 servings

*1¾ pounds (800 grams) or 1 package dry black turtle beans*
*2 tablespoons (30 millilitres) olive oil*
*½ cup (120 millilitres) onion, chopped*
*1½ cups (350 millilitres) leeks, chopped*
*6 cloves garlic, roughly chopped*
*water or vegetable stock, as needed*
*2 bay leaves*
*1 teaspoon (5 millilitres) cumin*
*¼ cup (60 millilitres) fresh parsley, chopped (or cilantro or scallions if preferred)*

Soak dry beans in water for 24 to 30 hours to soften. Preheat soup pot on medium-low heat, add olive oil and heat for 10 seconds. Add chopped onions and stir. Add chopped leeks and garlic. Stir for approximately 3 minutes. Strain presoaked beans, add to pot and stir. Add fresh water or vegetable stock to cover beans (approximately 1½ inches above beans). Add bay leaves and cumin. Simmer over moderate heat for approximately 45 minutes (or until beans feel soft enough when squeezed). Additional water/vegetable stock may be required during the cooking process to keep the beans covered with water. Once the beans are soft, remove the bay leaves and puree the beans in a food processor or with a hand blender. If the consistency of the beans is too thick add more water or stock for easier straining. Strain the beans in a bowl, using a spoon and pressing the beans against the strainer for better results. Put pureed beans back into pot, on low heat, to achieve a velvety-smooth consistency. Just before serving, add chopped parsley, cilantro or scallions for a finishing touch.

The black turtle beans can be substituted with any other type of beans. If canned beans are used, you can skip the process of soaking and reduce the cooking time to 30 minutes.

# Loaded Potato Soup with Garlic, Leeks and Aged White Cheddar

*Lesley Stoyan, Co-founder, Dailey Apple and Apple Tree Markets Group*

Yield: 4 servings

*1 teaspoon (5 millilitres) garlic, minced*
*1 small onion, chopped*
*2 leeks, cleaned well and finely chopped*
*1 teaspoon (5 millilitres) olive oil*
*3½ cups (775 millilitres) peeled diced potato*
*3 cups (700 millilitres) vegetable stock*
*1 cup (240 millilitres) aged white cheddar cheese, shredded*
*1 cup (240 millilitres) milk (rice, cow or goat)*
*no-salt seasoning (NSS), fresh dill, salt, black pepper*
*sour cream (optional for topping)*
*2 tablespoons (30 millilitres) shredded cheese for topping (optional for topping)*
*organic tomatoes, diced (optional for topping)*
*green onions, chopped (optional for topping)*
*crisp smoked bacon or pancetta (optional for topping)*

Using a stockpot, sauté garlic, onions and leeks in oil at low-medium heat. When onions become translucent, add potatoes. Mix and sauté for several minutes. Add vegetable stock. Bring to a boil and then reduce heat to simmer. Cover for 20 or more minutes or until potatoes are soft. Puree with blender stick or conventional mixer. Add cheese, milk, NSS, herbs, salt and pepper. Simmer until cheese melts. Serve in bowls or fancy mugs. Top with small sprig of fresh parsley or dill and shredded cheese. Add desired toppings and dig in!

# RECIPES

## Papá Angelo Garlic Soup

*Massimo Capra, Chef, Mistura Restaurant*

*It's called Papá Angelo because this was one of my dad's favorite soups that he often made for the family, as we never threw any bread out but always transformed it into something else.*

Yield: 4 to 6 servings

*1 tablespoon (15 millilitres) butter*
*1 tablespoon (15 millilitres) olive oil*
*1 cup (240 millilitres) garlic cloves, thinly sliced*
*3 sprigs thyme*
*4 cups (950 millilitres) vegetable or chicken stock*
*3 cups (700 millilitres) stale bread, cubed*
*4 eggs*
*1 cup (240 millilitres) 35 percent cream*
*1 cup (240 millilitres) Parmigiano, grated*
*2 tablespoons (30 millilitres) Italian parsley, chopped*
*salt and pepper to taste*

Pour butter and oil into stockpot set to low heat, add sliced garlic and cook gently. Add thyme and cook to develop flavour; add stock and bread. Simmer gently for at least 30 minutes, using whisk to smooth soup. Whisk eggs with cream and cheese, add parsley and stir mixture into boiling soup. Immediately remove from burner and stir well. Serve piping hot.

# "To Cure What Ails" Roasted Garlic Soup

*Kerri Cooper, Roots of Health Nutrition and Meal Delivery*

*The secret to this soup is the quality local ingredients, high-gelatin chicken broth and the deeply roasted garlic. To benefit from garlic's cold and flu fighting properties, add one to two cloves of very finely chopped fresh raw garlic just before serving.*

4 cups (950 millilitres) onions, chopped
¼ cup (60 millilitres) high-vitamin, grass-fed butter (or the best better you can get your hands on)
2 tablespoons (30 millilitres) olive oil
2 cups (475 millilitres) carrots, chopped
2 cups (475 millilitres) celery, chopped
2 cups (475 millilitres) roasted garlic, packed*
6 cups (1400 millilitres) high-gelatin bone broth (chicken bones from healthy birds that have been slowly cooked for 12 to 24 hours to release the most minerals and gelatin and produce the most flavour)
2 cups (475 millilitres) water
1½ teaspoons (7 millilitres) sea salt
½ teaspoon (2 millilitres) freshly ground black pepper
1 tablespoon (15 millilitres) rice vinegar
10 sprigs of fresh thyme, picked and chopped

Using a large soup pot with a thick bottom, sauté onions in butter and oil on medium heat until caramelized, about 20 minutes. Add carrot and celery and cook an additional 15 minutes, stirring often. Add roasted garlic, stock and water and bring to boil. Reduce to simmer and cook until vegetables are soft. Using hand-held blender, purée soup until thick and creamy. Add salt, pepper, rice vinegar and fresh thyme. Cook for a few more minutes and purée some more. Add more stock or water to reach desired consistency and season to taste with additional salt, pepper and vinegar.

*Toss peeled garlic generously in olive oil and roast in oven, uncovered on parchment paper, at 350°F (175°C) for approximately 45 minutes, or until golden.

## APPETIZERS AND SIDE DISHES

### Chunky Tomato Garlic Tapenade

*Dinah Koo, Chef/Owner, Peapods to Chanterelles*

*I've used this tapenade for lamb burgers, fish, pasta and bruschetta. It's particularly great in the summer and fall.*

Yield: 4 servings

*2 cups (475 millilitres) grape cherry tomatoes, washed*
*6 plump garlic cloves peeled, chopped finely in a food processor*
*¼ cup (60 millilitres) extra virgin olive oil*
*¼ cup (60 millilitres) black olives, chopped*
*1 to 2 teaspoons (5 to 10 millilitres) fresh basil or rosemary, chopped*
*pinch of salt to taste*

Toss tomatoes, garlic and oil in a medium-size bowl. Spread onto a parchment-lined pan. Roast in oven preheated to 400°F (200°C) for approximately 10 minutes. Stir once or twice. Tomatoes should be hot, blistered and wilted. Allow to cool. Add olives and basil (or rosemary). Will keep refrigerated for up to one week.

## Deviled Turnip with Garlic

*Peter McClusky, Garlic Farmer*

Yield: 8 servings

*2 large eggs, hard-boiled*
*2 tablespoons (30 millilitres) mayonnaise*
*½ teaspoon (2 millilitres) Dijon mustard*
*1 clove Ontario garlic, minced*
*⅛ teaspoon (0.6 millilitre) cayenne*
*salt and pepper to taste*
*4 hakurei turnips, about 2 inches (5 centimeters) in diameter, washed in cold water*
*paprika, as garnish*

Mash eggs in bowl with fork. Add mayonnaise, mustard, garlic and cayenne and stir with fork until smooth. Season with salt and pepper. Place covered in refrigerator. Cut each turnip in half lengthwise. Hollow out halves using a paring knife or a small spoon. Spoon mixture into each turnip half. Garnish with paprika. Keep covered in refrigerator until ready to serve.

Substitute garlic greens (2 tablespoons, finely chopped) or scapes (1 tablespoon, very finely chopped; woody parts removed) for bulbs.

## Garlic Chips

*Wayne Morris, Chef, Boralia*

*1 large bulb of garlic (the bigger the clove, the nicer the chip)*
*3 cups (700 millilitres) milk*
*2 cups (475 millilitres) neutral oil, such as grapeseed or canola*

Slice garlic on mandolin slicer or with knife to 1/25th inch (1 millimetre) in thickness. Bring milk to a boil and blanch sliced garlic for 10 seconds. Strain and reserve milk for other use. Repeat two more times with fresh milk each time. Pat garlic slices dry. Heat oil to 300°F (150°C). Fry garlic in oil until light golden colour and remove with spatula onto paper towel. Season with salt.

# Garlic and Cream Beans

*Corey Mintz, Food Writer, Toronto Star*

*Every other time I go to write a recipe, I question the use of confit garlic. It's the sort of prepared ingredient—just garlic simmered in oil until it's golden and spreadable—found in most professional kitchens, prepared in large batches. Except that it's not in every home kitchen. And readers, I've found, will only jump over one or two hurdles—an obscure ingredient, a new cooking method—before abandoning a recipe. I never want to use up a get-out-of-jail-free card on garlic. So this is a simple recipe (the other ingredients are just beans and cream) that will let you see how simple the confit step is. You can just make the four cloves you need for this recipe. But make a bigger batch. Keep refrigerated and use within one week.*

Yield: 4 servings

*4 cloves confit garlic, mashed*
*vegetable oil*
*½ cup (120 millilitres) 35 percent cream*
*4 cups (950 millilitres) navy beans, cooked*
*salt and pepper to taste*
*handful of fresh oregano or thyme*

To make confit garlic: Peel garlic cloves and trim ends. Cover with vegetable oil in small pot. Bring to low simmer and cook until cloves are golden, about 15 minutes. If you're making a large batch, cool and store in the fridge for later use.

In a large pan on medium heat, warm garlic, cream and beans. Reduce until beans are sticky, about 5 minutes. Season to taste with salt and pepper. Add herbs and serve.

# Mango or Green Apple Kuccha

*Vanesha Nuckchaddee-Khadaroo, Chef, La Marmite Mauricienne Catering*

Yield: 4 servings

*1 pound (450 grams) mango or green apple, cubed*
*½ cup (120 millilitres) garlic, coarsely cut*
*1 lime (for juice)*
*coarse sea salt*
*½ cup (120 millilitres) canola or vegetable oil*
*1 tablespoon (15 millilitres) mustard powder*
*1 tablespoon (15 millilitres) turmeric powder*
*2 tablespoons (30 millilitres) garlic, crushed*
*5 to 6 green chilies, coarsely cut (optional)*

Combine fruit, coarse cut garlic, lime juice and salt to taste. Place fruit on paper towel–covered plate for 3 to 4 hours to remove excess water. Or, in summer, cover with cloth and let dry in sun. Heat pan and add oil. Turn off burner. Add spices (including crushed garlic) and some salt. Add fruit and chilies. Mix well and add salt to taste. Leave kuccha overnight or 5 to 6 hours (marinating with spices), before serving.

Enjoy with rice, briani, roti or baguette as a side dish or salad.

# Oven-Roasted Squash with Smoked Garlic and Maple Syrup

*Bart Nagel, garlic farmer, Bulbs of Fire in Tiny, Ontario*

*Bart grows more than thirty-five varieties of garlic and smokes his own garlic.*

Prep time: 20 minutes
Cooking time: approximately 35 minutes
Needed equipment: 1 large baking pan

Yield: 6 servings

*1 medium-sized squash (butternut, acorn, buttercup are all great)*
*6 shallots*
*2 heads of smoked garlic (substitute with fresh garlic if no smoked available)*
*4 tablespoons (60 millilitres) olive oil*
*3 sprigs rosemary*
*½ cup (120 millilitres) maple syrup*
*1 cup (240 millilitres) walnuts (optional)*
*1 cup (240 millilitres) dried cranberries (optional)*
*½ pound (230 grams) bacon (optional)*

Preheat oven to 375°F (190°C). Peel squash and remove seeds. Cut squash in slices, approximately 1 inch (2½ centimeters) thick. Remove outer skin of shallots and cut in quarters. Peel (smoked) garlic.

Pour half of olive oil into a baking pan. Spread squash slices in pan and lay shallots and garlic cloves on top. Sprinkle remaining olive oil on top. Divide rosemary sprigs in the pan and finish off with maple syrup. Salt and pepper to taste. Optional additions for an extra-festive dish are walnuts, dried cranberries and slices of bacon over top. At Bulbs of Fire, we usually go all out!

Place baking pan in oven covered with aluminum foil for approximatly 35 minutes. Remove the cover for last 10 minutes and start checking squash for softness after 30 minutes.

## Roasted Beets with Almond-Potato Skordalia

*Peter Minaki, Kalofagas, Greek Food and Beyond*

*A skordalia is a Greek mashed puree. This dish is a play on a Greek favourite: roasted beet salad with lots of garlic. It is a popular side dish that creative types have created as a mash-up (pun intended) of a beet skordalia. Inspired by a dish from the Kokkari cookbook and restaurant in San Francisco, this roasted beet and skordalia is the perfect dish to serve alongside fried fish and seafood. A traditional skordalia is made with a mortar and pestle where either soaked day-old bread or boiled potatoes are pulverized with lots of garlic and emulsified with extra virgin olive oil.*

*One of the best skordalias I've tasted was at Artistou's Bakalarkia across from the Port of Thessaloniki. Aristou's skordalia was made of bread and mashed walnuts. My version of skordalia uses blanched almonds and boiled potatoes. When making a skordalia, use a mortar and pestle. Never use a mixer or food processor, unless you want wallpaper paste.*

Yield: 4 servings

*2 to 3 medium-sized beets*
*½ to ⅔ cup (120 to 160 millilitres) extra virgin olive oil, plus additional oil*
*sea salt*
*¼ to ⅓ cup (60 to 80 millilitres) red wine vinegar, plus 2 to 3 tablespoons (30 to 45 millilitres)*
*2 sprigs fresh thyme*

*2 large Yukon Gold potatoes*
*5 to 6 cloves of garlic, minced*
*½ cup (120 millilitres) almonds, blanched*
*scallions, sliced*
*blanched almond slices*

Preheat oven to 400°F (200°C). Place beets in centre of a large sheet of aluminum foil. Drizzle with olive oil. Tightly wrap beets in foil on baking sheet and place in oven for 30 minutes. Remove from oven and cool until still warm. Unwrap, discarding foil. Use back of knife to peel off skin and slice beets into wedges. Season with sea salt, extra virgin olive oil, red wine vinegar and fresh thyme leaves. Toss well and reserve. In the meantime, place your potatoes in a medium-size pot and fill with water. Add some salt and boil until fork tender. Strain and replace with cold water to help cool potatoes. Put garlic cloves, blanched almonds, coarse sea salt and a splash of wine vinegar into a mortar and mash into a paste with the pestle. As soon as potatoes are cool enough to handle, peel off skins with back of knife, quarter and add to paste in mortar. Mash with pestle. Add extra virgin olive oil in increments while mixing with pestle. Taste along the way, adding salt and red wine vinegar to taste. Serve potato/almond skordalia on a platter, topped with wedges of dressed beets. Spoon some of the beet juices on top and garnish with sliced scallions and sliced almonds. Serve with a mixed seafood platter. Garlicky skordalia and roasted beets are a perfect match to fried seafood. Wash it down with Ouzo or a crisp, white Greek wine.

## *Roasted Garlic*

*Donna Dooher, Chef, Mildred's Temple Kitchen*

*A lobster or escargot fork is great for extracting the garlic cloves from their roasted skins. It's delicious paired with a glass of Primitivo.*

Yield: 6 servings

*1 bulb garlic*
*¼ cup (60 millilitres) extra virgin olive oil*

Cut off top of garlic bulb, about a ¼ of the way down. Brush with a bit of olive oil and wrap in foil. Roast in oven preheated to 350°F (175°C) for approximately 25 minutes (time will vary depending on size of bulb). Remove foil. Place warm, soft garlic bulb on a large plate. Drizzle with olive oil. Serve with whipped sheep's ricotta, chèvre or any cheese of your liking, as well as grilled bread.

# RECIPES

## CONDIMENTS, SAUCES AND DRESSINGS

### *Garlic Scape Chimichurri*

*Emily Leonard, Casero Taco Bus*

*Chimichurri is a green sauce that originated in Argentina. It's such a wonderful summertime condiment, as you can easily whip up a batch using whatever combination of fresh herbs you have growing in your garden. And depending on the season, you can substitute and adjust the recipe—as we have done in our Garlic Scape Chimichurri recipe. Add a touch of acidity, citrus, oil and some spice, and you have a versatile, fresh sauce just begging to be served with charred meats and fish—or, as we do on the Taco Bus, on a fresh corn tortilla with whatever local meat or veg we've smoked or chargrilled!*

Prep time: 30 minutes
Yield: approximately 2 cups (475 millilitres)

*½ cup (120 millilitres) olive oil*
*4 tablespoons red wine vinegar*
*4 tablespoons fresh lime juice (or lemon juice)*
*6 garlic scapes, chopped (or garden-fresh garlic when scapes aren't available)*
*1 shallot, peeled and roughly chopped*
*½ teaspoon kosher salt*
*½ teaspoon freshly ground black pepper*
*½ teaspoon dried crushed red pepper flakes (or 1 whole seeded fresh chili pepper)*
*2 cups (475 millilitres) or 1 whole bunch fresh parsley, rough stems removed, washed and dried*
*1 cup (240 millilitres) or 1 whole bunch fresh cilantro, rough stems removed, washed and dried*
*1 cup (240 millilitres) fresh oregano*
*½ cup (120 millilitres) fresh mint, stems removed, rinsed*
*½ cup (120 millilitres) fresh epazote stems removed, rinsed (optional)*

In a food processor, combine all ingredients. Pulse until roughly blended, but still with some texture. Season to taste—add more vinegar or salt. Serve with chargrilled skirt steak or whole grilled fish.

# Garlic Scape and Ontario Honey Butter

*Alexandra Feswick, Chef du Cuisine, Drake Hotel*

*7½ ounces (225 grams) garlic scapes, chopped into ½-inch pieces*
*1 pound (450 grams) unsalted butter at room temperature*
*1 tablespoon (15 millilitres) fresh lemon juice*
*3 tablespoons (45 millilitres) local honey*
*¼ teaspoon (1 millilitre) cayenne pepper*
*1 teaspoon (5 millilitres) salt*

In food processer, add garlic scapes and pulse until roughly chopped. Add butter, lemon juice, honey, cayenne and salt. Blend until smooth and the ingredients are thoroughly combined (approximately 1 minute). Using a rubber spatula, remove butter from food processor and divide into three even piles. Roll out food film flat on the counter, leaving roll still intact. Add each pile of butter and smooth out until it becomes a flat mound. Cover with the food film approximately 6 inches long and 1 inch wide. Slowly and evenly roll the food film around the butter, creating a cylinder. Tie each end of food film to completely seal butter. Repeat with the remaining piles of butter.

Refrigerate for up to four days or freeze for enjoyment all year!

## Thunder Garlic Dressing

*Brad Long, Belong Café*

*This is a recipe with a lot of bite due to the high acid and garlic content. When tasting, it is best to use a piece of lettuce to get the most realistic final balance of flavours. Adjust salt to taste and enjoy.*

2 cups (475 millilitres) cold pressed sunflower, grapeseed or your favourite oil
¾ cup (180 millilitres) cider vinegar
1 cup (240 millilitres) freshly grated (rasped) Thunder Oak Cheese or your best local
　Gouda-style cheese, preferably aged 6 months to a year
1 tablespoon (15 millilitres) freshly puréed garlic
2 tablespoons (30 millilitres) braised garlic cloves
2 tablespoons roasted garlic
½ cup (120 millilitres) roasted garlic oil (or whatever's left after roasting the whole
　garlic heads)
1 ounce (30 millilitres) mushroom tea reduction
2 teaspoons (10 millilitres) Dijon mustard
juice of 1 lemon
salt to taste

Combine all ingredients in blender and puree. Serve.

*If allowed to sit overnight, the dressing will break (separate). This is okay and just requires vigorous stirring to come back to the proper creamy consistency. The seasoning should be pushed to the extreme, as salad leaves will be somewhat wet from washing, and this can dampen the impact. The garlic may be increased dramatically as per seasonal quality, and you can use variations of garlic preparation. Meaning you don't have to braise, roast and grate fresh, but doing so greatly improves the depth and breadth of flavour. Just use good, fresh garlic if you're feeling lazy or in a hurry. The cheese is extremely important because it adds the sweetness to soften the otherwise strong acid flavours and, along with the mushroom tea, delivers umami (a flavour descriptor for natural glutamates), bringing all the flavours to a peak. The mushroom stock has the same function in this dressing as anchovy performs in Caesar dressing—as a glutamic protein, it boosts the flavour without such volume that you taste mushroom (or anchovy in a balanced Caesar).*

# FISH AND SEAFOOD

## *Garlic Shrimp*

*Fred Staheli, Executive Chef (1988), Winston's Restaurant*
*Recipe provided by John Arena*

*Former Winston's owner John Arena recalled that this was the only dish with garlic served at Winston's, and it was served only once. The patron sent the dish back.*

Yield: 4 servings

*¼ cup (60 millilitres) extra virgin olive oil*
*1½ pound (675 grams) jumbo shrimp, peeled and deveined*
*salt and pepper to taste*
*2 large garlic cloves, very finely chopped*
*2 tablespoons (30 millilitres) small capers, drained*
*¼ cup (60 millilitres) fresh lemon juice*
*2 tablespoons (30 millilitres) Italian parsley, fresh and finely chopped*

In a large skillet, heat 2 tablespoons (30 millilitres) olive oil until shimmering. Season shrimp generously with salt and pepper. Add shrimp to skillet and cook over high heat until lightly browned and barely opaque, about 2 to 3 minutes. Before removing from heat, add garlic and capers. Remove from heat and add lemon juice and parsley. Serve it hot on warm dish.

# RECIPES

## *Skorthalia*

*James Chatto, Food and Restaurant Critic, Author*
*From* A Kitchen in Corfu, *by James Chatto and W.L. Martin (1987)*

*This recipe comes from my daughter's godmother, Koula Parginou, who lives in the remote village of Loutses on the Greek island of Corfu. She prepares skorthalia when she is making the traditional dish of salt cod and potatoes, after soaking the salt cod in cold water overnight to get rid of the salt and reconstitute the fish and then setting the cod to boil with six potatoes, peeled and cut into bite-sized pieces. When the potatoes are soft, she removes eight or nine pieces and puts them in a saucer. Then she takes two large heads of garlic, breaks them up into cloves, peels them, and mashes them to a pulp with a pestle and mortar.*

*With the scent of the garlic and fish mingling tantalizingly in the kitchen, Koula makes her skorthalia, dropping the potato, bit by bit, into the mortar as she continues to pound, and dribbling in a little of her best olive oil at frequent intervals. The process takes 10 minutes, for Koula is thorough, and uses about ⅓ cup of oil. At the end, she is left with a bowl of warm, creamy sauce, slightly fragrant and salty from the potato's liaison with the cod, and pungently hot from the garlic. The fish and remaining potatoes are drained and served up beside a heap of green beans, quickly boiled and still firmish, with three or four tablespoons of skorthalia between them. As a last touch, Koula dribbles a little more fresh oil over everything. Half a loaf of soft white bread completes the meal. A potato sauce over potatoes might seem like gilding the lily, but it is a delicious lunch, and besides, in a good skorthalia the identity of the potatoes vanishes during the long pulverization. Skortho means garlic, after all—not potato!*

# RECIPES

## Tosa-Style Garlic Salmon Sashimi

*Sang Kim, Restaurateur, Windup Bird Café, Blowfish; Chef, "Sushi Making for the Soul" workshops*

*I created this "Tosa-style" (bonito-infused soy sauce) garlic salmon sashimi. Although garlic was not traditionally a staple of the Japanese diet, it was in the former province of Tosa that its farming residents discovered their love for the plant. A spoon makes an ideal serving vessel.*

Prep time: 10 minutes
Cooking time: 12 hours, including marinating time
Yield: 8 servings

*3 teaspoons (5 millilitres) mirin (sweet rice wine)*
*2 tablespoons (30 millilitres) rice vinegar*
*1 tablespoon (15 millilitres) soy sauce*
*2 tablespoons (30 millilitres) bonito flakes*
*1 teaspoon (5 millilitres) fresh lime juice*
*2 cloves garlic, minced*
*1 pound (450 grams) salmon fillet, skinned*
*½ cup (120 millilitres) Spanish onion, finely chopped*

Combine mirin, vinegar, soy sauce and bonito flakes in a saucepan and bring to boil. Remove from heat and cool. Pour sauce through a strainer into a bowl; discard bonito flakes. Add lime juice and garlic. Slice pieces of salmon along the grain, ½ inch thick and 1 inch long. Marinate in fridge for up to 12 hours. Serve salmon scattered with onion.

# MEAT

## *Pahari Chicken*

*Aman S. Patel*

*This recipe was shared by Aman Patel, son of the late chef Amar Patel, who founded Indian Rice Factory in 1970, when authentic Indian food was scarce.*

Yield: 6 servings

*4 tablespoons (60 millilitres) ghee or cooking oil of your choice*
*6 cardamom pods*
*2 inches (5 centimetres) of ginger, pureed or finely chopped*
*4 cloves garlic, pureed or finely chopped*
*8 fresh green chilies or 1 teaspoon red chilies, ground*
*1 medium chicken, cut or equivalent in boneless chicken*
*3 cups (750 millilitres) yogurt, whipped*
*salt to taste*
*½ teaspoon (2 ½ centimetres) garam masala*
*¼ cup (60 millilitres) coriander, chopped (for garnish)*

Heat ghee or oil until hot. Add cardamom pods, ginger and garlic and fry for approximately 1 minute. Add chilies and continue to fry for approximately another ½ minute. Add chicken and brown. Add yogurt, lower heat and simmer until chicken is cooked. Add salt to taste. Sprinkle garam masala. Pour into serving bowl and garnish with coriander.

RICE PREP
*1 cup Basmati rice*
*2 cups water*
*½ cup green peas*
*½ cup cauliflower*
*½ cup cabbage, chopped*
*½ teaspoon butter*
*pinch of salt to taste*

Wash rice and drain. Bring water to boil in pot; add rice and all vegetables. Bring to vigorous boil. When water boils down to level of rice, cover and turn down heat to low for approximately 10 to 15 minutes. Remove from heat and set aside. Add butter prior to service.

# Roasted Capon with Sardinian Stuffing

*Rita DeMontis*

*My mother was so careful with garlic, but she had this one dish that was so delicious! It's two recipes in one: Roasted Capon with Sardinian Stuffing. It's part of my Sardinian heritage. The aroma of garlic, parsley and rosemary will drive you nuts!*

Yield: 4 servings

*olive oil*
*1 fresh capon, about 3 to 4 pounds (1.3 to 1.8 kilograms)*
*Sardinian stuffing*
*1 pound (450 grams) Yukon Gold potatoes, peeled and cut in quarters*
*2 cloves garlic*
*¼ cup (60 millilitres) fresh parsley, chopped*
*2 leaves fresh basil*
*1 tablespoon (15 millilitres) dried rosemary leaves*
*olive oil*
*salt/pepper to taste*

Rub some olive oil over capon. Stuff with Sardinian stuffing (recipe to follow) and place in a roasting pan big enough to hold chicken and potatoes. Sprinkle potatoes all around chicken. Mix garlic, parsley, basil and rosemary leaves together and sprinkle over chicken and potatoes. Drizzle olive oil over everything. Cover and bake in 350°F (175°C) for about an hour, removing cover and low-grilling capon and potatoes to give them a bit of crunch (do not overbake). Serve with stuffing on side, seasonal vegetables and a salad.

### SARDINIAN STUFFING

*This is my family's favourite. What makes this stuffing so interesting is the use of chicken livers and hot capicola Italian cold cuts…and the fact you can slice the stuffing after it's baked. This recipe is good for one medium turkey or one large capon.*

*3 tablespoons (45 millilitres) olive oil*
*1 clove garlic, minced*
*2 tablespoons (30 millilitres) flat Italian parsley, finely chopped*
*8 chicken livers, including liver found in cavity of bird, membranes removed, coarsely chopped*
*20 slices hot capicola deli meat, coarsely chopped*
*4 eggs*
*½ cup (125 millilitres) milk*
*1½ cups (375 millilitres) fine bread crumbs*
*salt and pepper to taste*
*pinch nutmeg*

In a large fry pan, heat olive oil. Sauté garlic and parsley until the garlic is translucent. Add chicken livers and stir quickly, 3 to 5 minutes (livers should still be on pink side). Remove from heat. Add chopped capicola and blend. Cool slightly. Add eggs one at a time, milk and bread crumbs. Season with salt and pepper and pinch of nutmeg. Gently stuff bird; cover opening with layer of aluminum foil. When bird is done, transfer to a warm platter and keep warm, lightly covered with foil. Gently remove stuffing whole and slice as you would a meatloaf.

# RECIPES

## Roasted Chicken "Peruvian Style" with Garlic and Herbs Marinade

*Elizabeth Rivasplata, Executive Chef, Rogers Centre/Toronto Blue Jays*

Yield: 6 servings

*4 cup (950 millilitres) fresh mint leaves*
*3 tablespoons (45 millilitres) extra virgin olive oil*
*10 garlic cloves, coarsely chopped*
*1 tablespoon (15 millilitres) salt*
*1 tablespoon (15 millilitres) pepper*
*1 tablespoon (15 millilitres) ground cumin*
*1 tablespoon (15 millilitres) sugar*
*2 teaspoons (5 millilitres) smoked paprika*
*2 teaspoons (10 millilitres) dried oregano*
*2 teaspoons (10 millilitres) grated lime zest, plus ¼ cup juice (2 limes)*
*1 teaspoon (10 millilitres) habanero chili, minced (or chili of your preference)*
*1 3½- to 4-pound (1.5 to 1.8 kilograms) whole chicken, giblets discarded*

Process mint, oil, garlic, salt, pepper, cumin, sugar, paprika, oregano, lime zest and juice, and habanero in blender until a smooth paste forms, 10 to 20 seconds. Use fingers to gently loosen skin on chicken covering breast and thighs. Place half of paste under skin, directly on meat of breast and thighs. Gently press skin to distribute paste over meat. Spread entire exterior surface of chicken with remaining paste. Tuck wings behind back. Place chicken in 1-gallon zip-lock bag and refrigerate for 6 to 24 hours, turning every 3 to 4 hours to make sure marinade spreads all over chicken.

Adjust oven rack to lowest position and heat oven to 325°F (160°C). Place vertical roaster on rimmed baking sheet. Slide chicken onto vertical roaster so drumsticks reach down to bottom of roaster, chicken stands upright and breast is perpendicular to bottom of pan. Roast chicken until skin just begins to turn golden and breast registers 140°F (60°C), 45 to 55 minutes. Carefully remove chicken and pan from oven and increase oven temperature to 500°F (260°C).

Once oven has come to temperature, place 1 cup water in bottom of baking sheet and continue roast until entire chicken skin is browned and crisp and breast registers 160°F (70°C) and thighs 175°F (80°C), about 20 minutes, rotating baking sheet halfway through roasting. Check chicken halfway through roasting; if top is becoming too dark, place 7-inch-square piece of aluminum foil over neck and wingtips of chicken and continue to roast. (If pan begins to smoke and sizzle, add additional water.) Carefully remove chicken from oven and let rest, still on vertical roaster, for 20 minutes. Using two large wads of paper towels, carefully lift chicken off vertical roaster and onto carving board to rest. Carve and serve.

## Smoked & Cracked's Roasted Garlic Smoked Beef Brisket

*Ron Raymer, Chef, Smoked & Cracked*
*Start recipe four days prior to serving*

Yield: 6 servings

*1 7- to 8-pound (3 to 3.5 kilograms) beef brisket, trimmed*

INGREDIENTS FOR RUB
*2 tablespoons (30 millilitres) chili powder*
*2 tablespoons (30 millilitres) salt*
*3 cloves fresh garlic, chopped*
*1 finely onion, chopped*
*1 tablespoon (15 millilitres) ground black pepper*
*1 tablespoon (15 millilitres) brown sugar*
*1 tablespoon (15 millilitres) Dijon mustard*

*3 pints (1.4 litres) Cameron's 266 dark lager or other dark beer*
*2 pounds (900 grams) fresh Ontario garlic, roasted and peeled*
*freshly ground black pepper*
*3 medium onions, roughly chopped*
*2 carrots, peeled and roughly chopped*
*2 stalks celery, roughly chopped*
*¼ cup (60 millilitres) apple cider vinegar*
*1 tablespoon (15 millilitres) lemon juice*
*4 tablespoons (60 millilitres) chipotle peppers*
*2 cup (475 millilitres) Smoked & Cracked's smoked tomato ketchup (or other tomato ketchup)*
*4 fresh tomatoes, roughly chopped*
*½ cup (120 millilitres) molasses*
*½ cup (120 millilitres) brown sugar*
*1 tablespoon (15 millilitres) Worcestershire sauce*
*1 teaspoon (5 millilitres) salt*
*1 teaspoon (5 millilitres) cayenne (optional)*

Make dry rub by combining chili powder, salt, garlic, onion, black pepper, brown sugar and Dijon mustard. Season raw brisket on both sides with rub. Place in dish, cover, put in the fridge for 2 days. Put brisket in smoker and smoke at 220°F (100°C) for 4 hours. Combine rest of ingredients. Put beef in slow cooker or suitable oven pan with lid. Cover with ingredient mixture. Cook in slow cooker or a 250°F oven (make sure pan is sealed with lid or foil wrap) for 9 to 11 hours. Remove beef and let stand. Blend all remaining ingredients in blender until smooth. Slice brisket, pour on sauce…and salivate!

# RECIPES

## Vegetarian

### Cabbage, Carrots and Potatoes (Tikil Gomen)

*Chef Banche Kinde (Rendezvous Restaurant) with Chef Michael Kidus (Dukem Restaurant)*

*Serve this Ethiopian dish with injera, a unique, traditional sourdough flatbread with a spongy texture from Ethiopia and Eritrea. French bread can be used in place of injera.*

Yield: 4 servings

*½ cup (125 millilitres) canola oil*
*1½ medium yellow onions, halved, thinly sliced*
*3 large carrots, peeled, thinly sliced*
*2 white potatoes, peeled, cut in 1-inch cubes*
*1 tablespoon (15 millilitres) fresh garlic, minced*
*1 teaspoon (5 millilitres) fresh ginger, minced*
*¼ teaspoon (1 millilitre) turmeric*
*¼ teaspoon (1 millilitre) fine sea salt*
*¼ teaspoon (1 millilitre) black pepper*
*1 cup (250 millilitres) water*
*8 to 10 cups (2 to 2.3 litres) green cabbage, chopped*
*1 jalapeño, chopped, with seeds*

In a 10-inch saucepan, heat oil to medium. Add onion. Cook, stirring, for 4 minutes. Add carrots. Cook, stirring, for 4 minutes. Add potatoes. Cover. Cook for 5 minutes. Add garlic, ginger, turmeric, salt and pepper. Cook, stirring, for 1 minute. Add water and cook, stirring, for 3 minutes. Add cabbage and jalapeño. Cook, stirring, for 1 minute. Cover and cook, stirring occasionally, until vegetables are soft, about 5 to 8 minutes.

Serve with Yellow Split Peas with Turmeric Sauce (Yekik Alicha); see recipe following.

# Yellow Split Peas with Turmeric Sauce (Yekik Alicha)

*Chef Banche Kinde (Rendezvous Restaurant) with Chef Michael Kidus (Dukem Restaurant)*

Yield: about 3 cups (750 millilitres)

*1 cup (250 millilitres) dried yellow split peas, washed*
*¼ cup (60 millilitres) canola oil*
*1½ medium yellow onions, finely minced*
*1½ tablespoons (22 millilitres) puréed fresh garlic, minced*
*1½ tablespoons (22 millilitres) fresh ginger, minced*
*½ teaspoon (2 millilitres) turmeric*
*3 cups (750 millilitres) water, plus more if needed*
*¾ teaspoon (4 millilitres) fine sea salt, or to taste*
*thinly sliced jalapeños with seeds (optional garnish)*
*red bell pepper, finely chopped (optional garnish)*

Place split peas in medium saucepan. Cover with water. Bring to boil over high heat. Boil 5 minutes. Let sit in water until ready to use. Drain. In medium saucepan, heat oil to medium. Add onions. Cook, stirring, for 8 minutes. Add garlic and ginger. Cook, stirring, for 1 minute. Stir in turmeric and then the drained split peas. Cook, stirring, for 1 minute. Add 3 cups (750 millilitres) water. Raise heat to high and bring to boil. Cook, stirring occasionally and adding more water if needed, until split peas are very soft and stew is thick and not soupy, about 30 minutes. Taste; season with salt.

If desired, serve garnished with jalapeños and bell peppers. Serve with Cabbage, Carrots and Potatoes (Tikil Gomen).

## Provision Rosetta Style

*Curt Hospidales, Chef, Hothouse Restaurant*

*Growing up in Trinidad, garlic was the meat in the pot.*

Yield: 6 servings

*4 pounds (1.8 kilograms) provision: any combo of potato, white yam, cassava or eddoes, cut in 2-inch cubes*
*vegetable oil for frying*
*5 cloves garlic*
*1 large onion, chopped*
*½ scotch bonnet pepper seeded, diced fine (adjust to personal heat preference)*
*½ red bell pepper, diced fine*
*salt and pepper to taste*

Boil provision in salted water until you can pierce with fork. Drain water and let dry a bit. While the provision boils, prepare other ingredients. When all are assembled and ready, heat a frying pan with oil coating the bottom. Drop in a bread cube to indicate when the oil is hot (when it begins to brown).

Now you can begin. Sauté garlic until lightly brown. Add onion. Sauté for 1 minute and then add provision and peppers. Toss in pan until all is blended; add salt and pepper to taste.

# RECIPES

## Historic Recipes

### Spiced Scallop Crudo

*We found this recipe in a book on native foods and wild plants that were used for medicinal and cooking purposes. The Mikma'q diet was predominantly seafood, and they would have used the wild garlic (also known as Canada onion or Canadian garlic). It grows naturally grows along the coastal shores. We found wild garlic growing right outside Port Royal, Nova Scotia, home of the first European settlement in Canada in 1605.*

ORIGINAL RECIPE

*raw spiced scallops*
*3 dozen bay scallops, shelled*
*2 tablespoons (30 millilitres) sunflower oil*
*1 clove garlic, chopped*
*1 small onion, diced*
*4 bay leaves*
*1 cup (240 millilitres) cider vinegar*

Combine all ingredients and chill overnight. Serve over chopped fresh parsley, dillweed and mint leaves.

MODERN EQUIVALENT (FERMENTED CHILI)
*Chef Wayne Morris, Boralia*

*Since it's hard to ferment a small quantity of chili, the recipe is for 30 servings.*

*14 ounces (400 grams) piment d'espelette or other medium-spice chili*
*14 ounces (400 grams) water*
*1½ teaspoons (8 millilitres) salt*
*2 cloves garlic, smashed*
*1¼ ounces (30 grams) late harvest apple cider vinegar*
*1¾ ounces (50 grams) shallots, minced*
*150 medium scallops*

Combine piment d'espelette, water, salt and garlic in a sterilized jar. Cover with cheesecloth and secure with rubber band. Allow to ferment at room temperature for 2 weeks. Strain off liquid and reserve. Combine fermented chili liquid with apple cider vinegar and shallot and blend.

Slice raw scallops thinly, season with salt and lay on a platter. Pour enough of the chili liquid to coat each piece of scallop lightly. Drizzle with sunflower oil. Garnish with garlic or chive flowers, sorrel leaves and garlic chips. (See recipe for garlic chips, page 110.)

## "To Dress Eggs with Garlic"

*Mess Establishment, Officers Brick Barracks, Fort York National Historic Site*
*From* The French Family Cook: Being a Complete System of French Cookery, *Menon (1744)*

ORIGINAL RECIPE

> *Boil ten cloves of garlic half a quarter of an hour in water; pound them with two anchovies and some capers, and then mix them with some oil, a little vinegar, salt and pepper; put this sauce into the bottom of your dish, and some eggs boiled hard, and properly arranged over it.*

MODERN EQUIVALENT

Yield: 10 to 12 appetizer-sized servings

*10 garlic cloves*
*4 to 5 anchovy fillets*
*10 capers*
*3 tablespoons (45 millilitres) extra virgin olive oil*
*4 teaspoons (20 millilitres) white wine vinegar*
*1 pinch of salt*
*½ teaspoon (2 millilitres) black pepper*
*10 eggs, hard-boiled*

Boil garlic cloves in water for approximately 15 minutes. Remove from heat, drain and allow to cool. Add anchovies, capers, olive oil, white wine vinegar, salt, pepper and cooled garlic cloves to a food processor and roughly blend. Spread mixture on serving plate and attractively arrange quartered or sliced hard-boiled eggs on top.

# RECIPES

## "To Make Paco-Lilla, or Indian Pickle, the Same the Mangoes Come Ever In"

*Mess Establishment, Officers Brick Barracks, Fort York*
*From Hannah Glasse's* The Art of Cookery Made Plain and Easy *(Hamden, CT: Archon Books, 1971), with an introduction by Fanny Craddock*

ORIGINAL RECIPE

*Take a pound of race-ginger, and lay it in water one night; then scrape it, and cut it in thin slices, and put to it some salt, and let it stand in the sun to dry; take long-pepper two ounces, and do it as the ginger. Take a pound of garlic, and cut it in thin slices, and salt it, and let it stand three days; then wash it well, and let it be salted again, and stand three days more; then wash it well, and drain it, and put it in the sun to dry; take a quarter of a pound of mustard-seeds bruised, and half a quarter of ounce of turmerick, put these ingredients, when prepared, into a large stone or glass jar, with a gallon of very good white wine vinegar, and stir it very often for a fortnight, and tie it up close. In this pickle you may put white cabbage, cut in quarter and put in a brine of salt and water for three days, and then boil fresh salt and water, and just put in the cabbage to scald, and press out the water, and put it in the sun to dry, in the same manner as you do cauliflowers, cucumber, melons, apples, French beans, plums, or any sort of fruit. Take care they are well dried before you put them into the pickle: you need never empty the jar, but as the things come in season, put them in, and supply it with vinegar as often as there is occasion. If you would have your pickle look green, leave out the turmerick, and green them as usual, and put them into this pickle cold. In the above, you may do walnuts in a jar by themselves; put the walnuts in without any preparation, tied close down, and kept some time.*

*For Your Kitchen:*

| Metric | Ingredient | Imperial | Original Recipe |
|---|---|---|---|
| 700 millilitres | fresh ginger, peeled and sliced | 3 cups | 1 pound |
| 550 millilitres | fresh garlic, peeled and sliced | 2¼ cups | 1 pound |
| 80 millilitres | black pepper, whole | ⅓ cup | 2 ounces |
| 250 millilitres | salt, kosher (for salting the ginger and garlic) | 1 cup | |
| 180 millilitres | mustard seed, whole | ¾ cup | ¼ pound |

| _Metric_ | _Ingredient_ | _Imperial_ | _Original Recipe_ |
|---|---|---|---|
| 7.5 millilitres | turmeric, ground | 1½ teaspoon | ½ ounce |
| 4 litres | white wine vinegar | 16 cups | 1 gallon |
| 1 | cabbage, whole, small | 1 | |
| 1 | cauliflower, whole, small | 1 | |
| 16 | cucumbers, small, pickling | 16 | |
| ½ | melon, honeydew | ½ | |
| 5 | apples, peeled, cored, cut in eighths | 5 | |
| 5 | plums, small, pitted and quartered | 5 | |
| 1 litres | green beans, trimmed and frenched | 4 cups | |
| 4 litres | water | 17 cups | |
| 1.2 litres | salt, kosher (for the brine) | 5 cups | |

_For the Pickle:_
Peel and slice garlic. Place in a ceramic bowl and add ⅓ cup (75 millilitres) salt. Cover with cheesecloth. Set in window in the sun to dry for three days. On the third day the garlic is drying, soak the ginger overnight in water. The next day, peel and cut ginger into thin slices. Place in a ceramic bowl and strew ⅓ cup (75 millilitres) salt over ginger. Cover with cheesecloth. Also on that same day, wash, drain and add remaining ⅓ cup (75 millilitres) salt to garlic. Dry both bowls of garlic and ginger in the sun for another three days. On the fourth day in a gallon jug, add to the wine vinegar the bruised mustard seeds, black pepper, turmeric, sun dried garlic and ginger. Cover tightly and refrigerate. Stir pickle daily for 2 weeks.

_For the Fruits and Vegetables:_
Prepare brine by mixing 17 cups water with 5 cups salt. Place quartered cabbage, cauliflower, green beans, cucumbers, melon, plums and apples in brine. Cover weight if necessary and refrigerate for 3 days. Drain fruits and vegetables from brine. Boil fresh salt water and put in vegetables and fruit, just to scald. Remove, and drain. Allow to dry at least 4 hours. Put the fruits and vegetables into pickle. Prepare jars. Fill jars with India pickle and seal. Keep for at least 4 months before opening.
>                   _Yield: 5 or 6 quarts (5 or 6 litres) of pickle_

## Desserts

# Black Garlic Brownies

*Chef Anne Sorrenti*
*Adapted from David Lebovitz's "Absolute Best Brownies" recipe (Leite's Culinaria)*

Yield: 9 to 12 brownies

*6 tablespoons unsalted or salted butter (plus more to grease foil)*
*4 ounces (110 grams) semisweet chocolate*
*4 ounces (110 grams) milk chocolate chips*
*¾ cup (180 millilitres) sugar*
*1 teaspoon vanilla extract*
*2 large eggs, room temperature*
*\*7 cloves of black/fermented garlic, chopped fine*
*¼ cup (60 millilitres) all-purpose flour*

Preheat oven to 350°F (175°C). Line 8-inch square pan with foil or parchment, lightly buttered and extending over the pan's edges. Melt butter in medium saucepan over low heat. Add chocolate and stir by hand until melted and smooth. Remove saucepan from heat. Stir in sugar and vanilla until combined. Beat in eggs by hand, one at a time. Stir in garlic. Add flour and stir energetically for 1 full minute, until batter loses its graininess, is smooth and glossy and begins to pull away from sides of saucepan. Scrape batter into prepared pan and bake until centre feels almost set, about 30 minutes. Do not overbake. Remove from oven. Let brownies cool completely in pan. While carefully holding foil or parchment, lift block of brownie out of the pan. Cut into squares. Brownies will keep well up to 4 days and can be frozen up to 1 month.

*If black/fermented garlic unavailable, substitute roasted garlic.

# Black Garlic Butter Tarts

*Ron Raymer, Chef, Smoked & Cracked*

Yield: 12 2-inch tarts

PASTRY
*1 pound (450 grams) lard*
*½ teaspoon (2 millilitres) salt*
*4 cups (950 millilitres) flour, sifted*
*1 egg, separated*
*1 cup (240 millilitres) lemonade*
*lemon rind*

FILLING
*¾ cup (180 millilitres) brown sugar*
*1 cup (240 millilitres) corn syrup*
*2 eggs*
*⅛ pound (125 millilitres) unsalted butter, softened*
*1 teaspoon (5 millilitres) vanilla extract*
*pinch salt*

APPLES, BROWNED
*1 tablespoon (15 millilitres) butter*
*1 tablespoon (15 millilitres) brown sugar*
*¼ teaspoon (1 millilitres) cinnamon*
*1 Granny Smith apple, cored and sliced*

OTHER FILLINGS AND GARNISH
*36 pecan halves*
*⅜ cup (90 millilitres) raisins*
*4 cloves black garlic, sliced*
*4 ounces (115 grams) dark unsweetened bakers chocolate*

For pastry: Gently combine lard, salt and flour. Do not overwork. Beat egg yolk, add lemonade and lemon rind and whisk for a few seconds. Beat egg white until light and fluffy. Add yolk and lemonade mixture to the pastry, gently working it in. Add egg white and fold in. Form into ball. Cover and refrigerate for 1 hour.

For filling: While pastry is resting, combine brown sugar, corn syrup, eggs, butter, vanilla and salt in stainless steel bowl. Whisk until smooth. Set aside.

For apples: Melt butter with brown sugar and cinnamon in saucepan on low heat. Add apple and cook until slices are soft.

Roll out pastry and put in tart shells or muffin pans to desired thickness (¼-inch). Put 3 pecan halves on walls of each tart. Add 1 apple slice, 3 raisins and 1 black garlic slice to each tart. Fill tarts with butter/corn syrup mixture to edge. Do not overfill.

Bake at 375°F (190°C) approximately 30 minutes. Let cool. Remove tarts. Melt chocolate and then use to brush edges of tart. Drizzle remainder over tarts if desired. Serve.

# RECIPES

## Roasted Garlic Butter Tarts

*Tigchelaar Apple Orchard/Just a Cup Coffee*

*Tigchelaar Farm's favourite butter tarts are found only at the farm in Puslinch and at the Aberfoyle Farmers' Market.*

Yield: 12 tarts

BUTTER PASTRY
*1 cup (240 millilitres) Tenderflake (or other pure lard)*
*½ cup (120 millilitres) unsalted butter, softened*
*4 cups (950 millilitres) all-purpose flour*
*1½ teaspoons (2 millilitres) salt*
*¼ cup (60 millilitres) ice water mixed with 1 egg and 1½ teaspoons (7 millilitres) apple cider vinegar*

Mix lard and butter into the flour with salt until blended into small corn-size pieces. Add water mixture all at once until just blended into a clump. Shape into disc and refrigerate for at least 1 hour. Roll pastry and place into 12 muffin tins.

FILLING FOR BUTTER TARTS
*½ cup (120 millilitres) butter*
*1 cup (240 millilitres) brown sugar*
*½ teaspoon (2 millilitres) salt*
*1½ teaspoons (7 millilitres) vinegar*
*1½ teaspoons (7 millilitres) vanilla*
*2 large eggs*
*1¼ cups (300 millilitres) corn syrup*
*⅓ cup (80 millilitres) caramelized garlic chips\**

Mix above ingredients until well blended. Fill tarts with filling. Cool garlic chips and add about ¼ to ½ teaspoon (1 to 3 millilitres), depending on how you feel about garlic! Bake in oven at 325°F (160°C) until golden brown.

\*Garlic, coarsely chopped and toasted in butter on stove until golden; add 1 tablespoon (15 millilitres) maple syrup.

## Dark Chocolate and Roasted Garlic Ice Cream

*Courtesy of Toronto Garlic Festival*
*Can be made with or without an ice cream machine.*

Yield: 6 servings

½ cup (120 millilitres) direct or fair trade bittersweet chocolate
4 cups (950 millilitres) 10 percent milkfat cream
8 large egg yolks
½ cup (120 millilitres) sugar
6 cloves Ontario garlic, roasted and mashed
2 teaspoons (10 millilitres) pure vanilla extract

Use whisk to combine chocolate and 1 cup cream in a 2-quart saucepan over medium heat. Add remaining cream. Bring mixture to simmer, stirring occasionally. Remove from heat. In a medium mixing bowl, whisk egg yolks until they lighten in colour. Gradually add sugar and whisk to combine. Slowly whisk ⅓ of the cream mixture into the egg yolks and sugar. Pour in remaining cream mixture while continuing to whisk. Return the mixed ingredients to the saucepan over low heat, stirring frequently, until the mixture thickens slightly and reaches 172°F (78°C). Add garlic. Pour mixture into container and let sit at room temperature for 30 minutes. Strain to remove garlic pulp. Stir in vanilla extract. Refrigerate for up to 8 hours or until temperature reaches 40°F (4°C) or below. Pour into an ice cream maker and process for approximately 30 minutes. Serve as is for a soft dessert or freeze for another 4 hours to allow ice cream to harden.

To make without an ice cream machine, remove container from freezer every 30 minutes, stir for 2 minutes and return to freezer until mixture reaches desired firmness.

# Garlic Brittle

*Kerri Cooper, Roots of Health Nutrition and Meal Delivery*

*Be sure to have a candy thermometer, parchment paper and pastry brush on hand when making this recipe.*

1½ cups (350 millilitres) cashews, chopped
1 cup (235 millilitres) almonds, chopped
½ cup (120 millilitres) roasted garlic\*, cut into small pieces
¾ cup (180 millilitres) organic corn syrup
3 cups (700 millilitres) sugar
¾ cup (180 millilitres) water
3 tablespoons (45 millilitres) unsalted butter
¼ teaspoon salt

Line one large baking sheet with parchment paper. Combine nuts and roasted garlic in a large bowl, coating the nuts with the garlic. Spread mixture as evenly as you can in one thin layer on the parchment paper. On medium heat in a small saucepan, add corn syrup, sugar and water. Attach candy thermometer to the side of the pot so the tip is inside the liquid but not touching the bottom of the pan. Do not stir. Bring mixture to a boil, brushing down the sides of pot with a pastry brush dipped in cold water, if needed. When mixture reaches 234°F (112°C) on a candy thermometer (approximately 10 minutes), check that it has reached softball stage (when you drop a bit of candy in cold water, it will form a soft ball, not a thread).

Stir in butter and salt and cook to 300°F (150°C) on a candy thermometer (approximately 10 minutes) or until it reaches hard crack stage (when you drop a bit of candy in cold water, it will form hard, brittle threads that crack when bent). Be careful not to burn yourself. Let candy cool in water for 1 minute to avoid burns. Add baking soda and mix for approximately 1 minute. The mixture will foam with the baking soda. Remove from heat and immediately pour hot sugar mixture over garlic/nut mixture on parchment-lined baking sheet. Working quickly and spread evenly with a spatula as best you can (this is easier with a kitchen partner); wait for brittle to cool until firm. Once cooled, break into pieces and enjoy!

\*Toss peeled garlic generously in olive oil and roast in oven, uncovered on parchment paper, at 350°F (175°C) for approximately 1 hour, until deeply golden.

*Appendix*

# USEFUL INFORMATION

GARLIC GROWERS ASSOCIATION OF ONTARIO promotes awareness of Ontario garlic with field trips and valuable information on growing, marketing and disease prevention. There is a nominal annual membership fee. garlicgrowers.on.ca.

The *GARLIC NEWS* is a valuable quarterly newsletter published by "Garlic Guru" Paul Pospisil (e-mail garlic@rideau.net to subscribe to his printed newsletter). garlicnews.ca.

The ONTARIO GARLIC MAP shows where to buy Ontario-grown garlic. Search "Ontario garlic map" online or at torontogarlicfestival.ca/where-to-buy-ontario-garlic.

The ONTARIO MINISTRY OF AGRICULTURE, FOOD AND RURAL AFFAIRS is the Ontario government ministry responsible for the food, agriculture and rural sectors of the Canadian province of Ontario and has information on Ontario garlic. omafra.gov.on.ca.

# CANADIAN GARLIC FESTIVALS

BRITISH COLUMBIA
Grindrod Garlic Festival. greencroftgardens.com/garlicfest.
Hills Garlic Festival. hillsgarlicfest.ca.
Pender Harbour Garlic Festival. facebook.com/PenderHarbourGarlicFestival.
South Cariboo Garlic Festival. garlicfestival.ca.

ALBERTA
Andrew Garlic Festival. andrewagsociety.com.

MANITOBA
Pembina Valley Honey Garlic and Maple Syrup Festival. rmofpembina.
com/honey-garlic.htm.

ONTARIO
Canadian Garlic Festival. canadiangarlicfestival.com.
Carp Garlic Festival. carpgarlicfestival.ca.
Eastern Ontario Garlic Festival. easternontariogarlicfestival.ca.
Garlic is Great Festival. newmarket.ca/en/GarlicisGreatFestivalEventPage.asp.
Haliburton County Garlic Fest. haliburtongarlic.ca.
Niagara Garlic Festival. niagaragarlicfestival.com.
Perth Garlic Festival. perthgarlicfestival.com.
Stratford Garlic Festival. stratfordgarlicfestival.com.
Toronto Garlic Festival. torontogarlicfestival.ca.
Verona Lions Garlic Festival. veronalions.ca/garlic-festival/general-info.

QUEBEC
Ste-Anne-de-Bellevue Garlic Festival. stannegarlicfestival.wordpress.com.

NOVA SCOTIA
Stinking Rose Garlic Festival. watershed farm.org.

# NOTES

## Introduction

1. Correspondence with Kirk Elliot, February 17, 2015.

## Chapter 1

2. Smith, *Oxford Companion to American Food and Drink*, 253.
3. Tsurumi, *Intellectual History of Wartime Japan*, 225.
4. Miller, "Identity Takeout," 431.
5. Correspondence with Salvatore LaGumina, director of the Center for Italian American Studies, Nassau Community College, Garden City, New York, December 30, 2014.
6. *It's a Wonderful Life*, Frank Capra, director, 1946, Liberty Films, United States.
7. Sturino and Zucchi, *Italians in Ontario*, 86.
8. Smith, "Why the Tomato Was Feared in Europe for More than 200 Years."
9. Lee et al., "Try It, You'll Like It," 1,054–58.
10. James, *Escoffier*, 70.
11. Correspondence with Cookie Roscoe, July 10, 2014.
12. Interview with James Chatto, November 28, 2014.
13. PubMed Health, "How Does Our Sense of Taste Work?"
14. Lakey, "They Say Spa-deenah."

## CHAPTER 2

15. Meredith, *Complete Book of Garlic*, 18.
16. Engeland, *Growing Great Garlic*, 35.
17. Young, *Ethnobotany*, 43.
18. Meredith, *Complete Book of Garlic*, 20.
19. Zohary et al., *Domestication of Plants in the Old World*, 156.
20. Meredith, *Complete Book of Garlic*, 20.
21. Musselman, *Figs, Dates, Laurel and Myrrh*, 144.
22. Lieberman, "Prehistoric Spices."
23. Block, *Garlic and Other Alliums*, 21.
24. Schutyser, *Caravanserai*, 8.
25. Oriental Express Central Asia, "Tash-Rabat Complex."
26. Waugh, "The Mongels."
27. At the time of writing, parts of old Kashgar are being demolished by the Chinese government.
28. *Economist*, "Kerala, India and the Molucca Islands," 51.

## CHAPTER 3

29. Duncan, *Canadians at Table*, 24.
30. Jaine, *Oxford Symposium on Food & Cookery*, 164.
31. Beckwith, *Historic Notes on the Northwest*, 88.
32. Small, *North American Cornucopia*, 199.
33. Moerman, *Native American Ethnobotany*, 54.
34. Kuhnlein and Turner, "Traditional Plant Foods," 79.
35. Sioui, *Huron-Wendat*, 111.
36. Litalien, *Champlain*, 141.
37. Gaston, *Order of Good Cheer*, 313.
38. Correspondence with Bridget Wranich, Programme Office, Fort York National Historic Site, August 3, 2012.
39. Burton and Cameron, *To the Gold Coast for Gold*, 334.
40. *Canada Presbyterian*, "Scientific and Useful," 471.
41. Driver, *Culinary Landmarks*, 274.
42. Ibid., 64.
43. Ibid., 288.
44. Traill, *Female Emigrants Guide*, 206.
45. Driver, *Culinary Landmarks*, xxii.
46. Hart, *Household Recipes or Domestic Cookery*, 17.

# CHAPTER 4

47. Historica Canada, "Immigration."

48. Riendeau, *Brief History of Canada*, 218.

49. Harris, Encyclopedia of Canada's Peoples/Peopling.

50. *Evening Star*, "Directions to Make a Genuine East Indian Chicken Curry," 5.

51. Driver, *Culinary Landmarks*, 276.

52. Ladies of Toronto and Chief Cities, *Home Cook Book*, 133.

53. Ibid., 134.

54. Ibid., 98.

55. Ibid., 95.

56. Ibid., 120.

57. Interview with Helena Moroz. December 2014.

58. Melville, letter, *Monthly Leaflet of the Canadian Congregational Woman's Board of Missions*, 6.

59. International Ladies Garment Workers Union Collection.

60. De Trey, "Dentist's Hygiene," 116.

61. Moore, "Medicinal Properties of Some Herbs and Garden Vegetables," 150.

62. Mackenzie, "Medicinal Treatment of Tuberculosis," 479.

63. *Catechism of Hygiene for the Use of Convents and Female Schools*, 21.

64. *Dominion Medical Monthly*, letter to the editor (December 1915).

65. Harney, Ancil and Ramirez, "Commerce of Migration," 25.

66. *Monetary Times, Trade Review and Insurance Chronicle*, "New Ontario," 309.

67. Beadle, *Canadian Fruit, Flower and Kitchen Gardener*, 226.

68. Canadian Institute of Ukrainian Studies, Internet Encyclopaedia of Ukraine.

69. Berton, *Promised Land*, 57.

70. Interview with Mary Stefura, December 4, 2014.

71. Interview with Sandra Sharko, December 4, 2014.

72. Interview with Mary Stefura, December 4, 2014.

73. Trustees' and Teachers Meeting, October 1, 1928.

74. Correspondence with Jean Gural, January 11, 2015.

75. Interview with Mike Murakami, October 25, 2014.

76. Contenta, Monsebraaten and Rankin, "Why Are So Many Black Children in Foster and Group Homes?" "We received a call because a child was sent to school with roti," said Danielle Mitchell, a child protection worker at Peel Children Aid's Society.

77. Interview with Sara Waxman, November 28, 2014.

78. Interview with Cookie Roscoe, May 21, 2014.

# CHAPTER 5

79. Desjardins and Desjardins, "Role of Food in Canadian Expressions of Christianity," 78.
80. Interview with Amy Morris, February 27, 2015.
81. Claiborne, "Art of French Cooking Does Not Concede to US Tastes."
82. Interview with Graham Kerr, November 19, 2014.
83. Interview with Richard Szpin, March 24, 2015.
84. Interview with Laurie Oehy, February 3, 2015.
85. Chatto, *Man Who Ate Toronto*, 111.
86. Newman, *Canadian Establishment*, 255.
87. Interview with Jason Huang, February 6, 2015.
88. John Arena has been growing his own garlic for many years, about five hundred plants annually. He shared a few bulbs with me that I planted and look forward to growing out.
89. Short, *I Must Say*, 5.
90. Interview with Dinah Koo, January 24, 2014.

# CHAPTER 6

91. Interview with David Cohlmeyer, February 7, 2014.
92. Interview with Greg Couillard, March 7, 2014.
93. Interview with Anne Sorrenti, January 14, 2015.
94. Ibid.
95. Ibid.
96. Correspondence with Marie Klassen, August 22, 2014.
97. Interview with Barry Gragg, January 6, 2015.

# CHAPTER 7

98. Interview with Mark Cullen, November 6, 2014.
99. Interview with Mary Stefura, December 7, 2014.
100. Interview with Ally Adams, January 11, 2015.
101. Interview with Wayne Greer, November 7, 2014.
102. Interview with Warren Ham, December 7, 2013.
103. Interview with Wayne Greer, November 7, 2014.
104. Interview with Mark Wales, November 4, 2012.
105. Elton, "About Time We Started Using Our Heads."
106. *Farmers' Markets Ontario*, "Impact Study."
107. Industry Canada, Canadian Importers Database, 2013 figures.
108. Interview with Suman Roy, February 26, 2015.

## Chapter 8

109. Interview with Dr. Eric Block, Chemistry Faculty, University at Albany, November 13, 2014.
110. Ibid.
111. Block, *Garlic and Other Alliums*, 84.
112. Tamaki, Kamati and Yamazaki, "Studies on the Deodorization by Mushroom Extract," 277–86.

## Chapter 9

113. Pizzorno, *Textbook of Natural Medicine*, 569.
114. Rivlin, "Historical Perspective on the Use of Garlic," 951S.
115. Aydin et al., "Antimicrobial Effects of Chopped Garlic," 204.
116. Correspondence with Bob Baloch, February 5, 2015.
117. Hobbs, "Garlic."
118. M'Farlane, "Foreign Bodies in the Auditory Canal," 173.
119. Interview with Harry Rosen, January 24, 2014.
120. Renoux, *For the Love of Garlic*, 119.
121. Lane, "New Light on Medicine," 84.
122. Block, *Garlic and Other Alliums*, 295.
123. Washburn, "Science's Worst Enemy."
124. Correspondence with Professor Jan Huizinga, Division of Gastroenterology, Department of Medicine, McMaster University, July 10, 2014.
125. Interview with Dr. Jackson, February 4, 2015.
126. Interview with Eric Block, December 9, 2014.

## Chapter 10

127. Tarrah Young, FarmStart Soil Workshop, May 2009.
128. Pospisil, "Growing Garlic from Bulbils," 14.
129. Interview with Patrick Carter, March 28, 2015.

## Chapter 11

130. Interview with Ed Burt, January 23, 2015.
131. Interview with Graham Kerr, November 19, 2014.
132. Interview with Michael Stadtländer, January 15, 2015.
133. *Goodfellas*, Martin Scorsese, director, 1990.
134. Interview with Curt Hospidales, November 26, 2014.

## CHAPTER 12

135. Canadian Food Inspection Agency, "Labeling Requirements for Processed Products."

## RECIPES

136. Correspondence with John Becker, February 27, 2015.
137. Rombauer and Rombauer, *Joy of Cooking*, 534.

# BIBLIOGRAPHY

A.B. of Grimsby. *The Frugal Housewife's Manual.* Toronto: J.H. Lawrence, 1840.

Alexander, Harry. *The Winston Dictionary for Canadian Schools.* Toronto: J.C. Winston, 1950.

Aydin, A., et al. "The Antimicrobial Effects of Chopped Garlic in Ground Beef and Raw Meatballs." *Journal of Medical Food* (March 10, 2007): 203–7. http://www.ncbi.nlm.nih.gov/pubmed/17472489.

Barr, Luke. *Provence 1970.* New York: Clarkson Potter, 2013.

Beadle, D.W. *Canadian Fruit, Flower and Kitchen Gardener.* Toronto: James Campbell & Son, 1872.

Beckwith, Hiram Williams. *Historic Notes on the Northwest.* Chicago: H.H. Hill and Company, 1879.

Berton, Pierre. *The Promised Land: Settling the West, 1896–1914.* Toronto: Doubleday Canada, 2011.

Block, Eric. *Garlic and Other Alliums: The Lore and the Science.* Cambridge, UK: Royal Society of Chemistry, 2010.

Burton, Richard, and Verney Cameron. *To the Gold Coast for Gold.* London: Chatto & Windus, 1883.

*Canada Presbyterian*, no. 30. "Scientific and Useful" (May 23, 1879): 471.

Canadian Food Inspection Agency. "Labeling Requirements for Processed Products. Country of Origin—Processed Products." http://inspection.gc.ca/food/labelling/food-labelling-for-industry/processed-products/eng/1393081288925/1393081317512?chap=7.

Canadian Institute of Ukrainian Studies. Internet Encyclopaedia of Ukraine. https://www.ualberta.ca/CIUS.

# BIBLIOGRAPHY

*Catechism of Hygiene for the Use of Convents and Female Schools, by a Teacher.* Quebec: Forgues & Wiseman, 1891.

Chatto, James. *The Man Who Ate Toronto.* Toronto: MacFarlane Walter & Ross, 1998.

Child, Julia. *My Life in France.* Toronto: Random House, 2006.

Claiborne, Craig. "Art of French Cooking Does Not Concede to US Tastes." *New York Times,* October 18, 1961.

Contenta, Sandro, Laurie Monsebraaten and Jim Rankin. "Why Are So Many Black Children in Foster and Group Homes?" *Toronto Star,* December 11, 2014. http://www.thestar.com/news/canada/2014/12/11/why_are_so_many_black_children_in_foster_and_group_homes.html.

Desjardins, Ellen, and Michel Desjardins. "The Role of Food in Canadian Expressions of Christianity." In *Edible Histories, Cultural Politics.* Edited by Franca Iacovetta, Valerie J. Korinek and Marlene Epp. Toronto: University of Toronto Press, n.d.

De Trey, E. "The Dentist's Hygiene." *Dominion Dental Journal* 4, no. 4 (July 1892): 112–19. http://eco.canadiana.ca/view/oocihm.8_04219_18/2?r=0&s=2.

*Dominion Medical Monthly.* Letter to the editor (December 1915).

Driver, Elizabeth. *Culinary Landmarks: A Bibliography of Canadian Cookbooks, 1825–1949.* Toronto: University of Toronto Press, 2008.

Duncan, Dorothy. *Canadians at Table: Food, Fellowship and Folklore: A Culinary History of Canada.* Toronto: Dundurn Press, 2006.

———. *Nothing More Comforting.* Toronto: Dundurn Group, 2003.

*The Economist.* "Kerala, India and the Molucca Islands, Indonesia" (December 18, 1998).

Elton, Sarah. "About Time We Started Using Our Heads." *MaClean's,* December 2, 2010. http://www.macleans.ca/culture/using-our-heads.

Engeland, Ron L. *Growing Great Garlic.* Okonagan: Filaree Productions, 1991.

*Evening Star.* "Directions to Make a Genuine East Indian Chicken Curry." Saturday, August 4, 1897.

*Farmers' Markets Ontario.* "Impact Study" (January 2009). http://www.farmersmarketsontario.com/Documents/FMO%20Impact%20Study%20-%20Overview%20and%20Highlights.pdf.

Francatelli, Charles Elme. *A Plain Cookery Book for the Working Classes.* N.p.: Tempus Publishing Limited, n.d.

Freedman, Roma. "A Breath-Taking Chew…That's Garlic!" *Ford Times* 64, no. 11 (November 1971). The Ford Motor Company.

Gaston, Bill. *The Order of Good Cheer.* Toronto: House of Anansi, 2009.

Hakutani, Yoshinobu, ed. *Theodor Dreiser's Uncollected Magazine Articles, 1897–1902.* Cranbury, NJ: Associated University Press, 2003.

Harney, Robert F., and Janet Hamilton. *Polyphony: The Bulletin of the Multicultural Society of Ontario* (Winter 1979). Toronto, Multicultural History Society of Ontario.

Harney, Robert F., Pierre Ancil and Bruno Ramirez. "The Commerce of Migration." *Canadian Ethnic Studies* 8 (1977): 42–53.

Harris, Lloyd J. *The Book of Garlic*. Berkeley, CA: Aris Books, 1979.

Harris, R. Cole. The Encyclopedia of Canada's Peoples/Peopling. Multicultural Canada. http://www.multiculturalcanada.ca.

Hart, Constance. *Household Recipes or Domestic Cookery*. Montreal: A.A. Stevenson, 1865.

Historica Canada. "Immigration." www.thecanadianencyclopedia.ca/en/article/immigration.

Hobbs, Christopher. "Garlic: The Pungent Panacea." Alternative Health, Wellness and Healthy Living Information. http://www.healthy.net/Health/Article/Garlic_The_Pungent_Panacea/881.

Iacovetta, Franca, Valerie Korinek and Marlene Epp. *Edible Histories, Cultural Politics: Towards a Canadian Food History*. Toronto: University of Toronto Press, 2012.

Industry Canada. Canadian Importers Database, 2013 figures. https://www.ic.gc.ca/eic/site/cid-dic.nsf/eng/home.

International Ladies Garment Workers Union Collection. http://multiculturalcanada.ca/node/266763.

Jaine, Tom. *Oxford Symposium on Food & Cookery, 1986: The Cooking Medium: Proceedings*. London: Prospect Books, 1987.

James, Kenneth. *Escoffier: The King of Chefs*. London: Hambledon and London, 2002.

Knox, John. *The Journal of Captain John Knox: An Historical Journal of the Campaigns in N. America for the Years 1757, 1758, 1759, and 1760 in Three Volumes*. Vol. 2. N.p.: Greenwood Press, 1968.

Kostick, Kenny. *Little Kenny in the Kitchen*. Toronto: Key Porter, 2002.

Kuhnlein, Harriet V., and Nancy J. Turner. "Traditional Plant Foods of Canadian Indigenous People: Nutrition, Botany and Use." *Food and Nutrition in History and Anthropology* 8 (1996).

Ladies of Toronto and Chief Cities and Towns in Canada. *The Home Cook Book*. Barrie, ON: Rose Publishing Company, 1887.

Lakey, Jack. "They Say Spa-deenah, but Are They Right?" *Toronto Star*, March 22, 2011. http://www.thestar.com/yourtoronto/the_fixer/2011/03/22/the_fixer_they_say_spadeenah_but_are_they_right.html.

Lane, Nick. "New Light on Medicine." *Scientific American* (January 2008): 80–87. doi:10.1038/scientificamerican0708-80sp.

Lee, Leonard, et al. "The Influence of Expectation, Consumption, and Revelation on Preferences for Beer." *Psychological Science* 17, no. 12 (2006).

———. "Try It, You'll Like It." *Psychological Science* 17, no. 12 (2006): 1,054–58.

Lieberman, Josh. "Prehistoric Spices: Neolithic Chefs Cooked with Garlic Mustard Before Development of Agriculture." *International Science Times* (August 22, 2013).

Litalien, Raymonde. *Champlain: The Birth of French America*. Montreal: McGill-Queen's University Press.

Macfarlane, James. *The Cook Not Mad*. Kingston, ON: Upper Canada, 1831.

Mackenzie, Hector. "The Medicinal Treatment of Tuberculosis." *Canadian Practitioner* 23, no. 8 (August 1898): 470–80. http://eco.canadiana.ca/view/oocihm.8_05187_236/23?r=0&s=1.

McGee, Harold. *Keys to Good Cooking*. Toronto: Doubleday Canada, 2010.

Melville, Helen J. Letter. *Monthly Leaflet of the Canadian Congregational Woman's Board of Missions* (January 1898).

Meredith, Ted Jordan. *The Complete Book of Garlic*. Portland, OR: Timber Press, 2008.

M'Farlane, Murray. "Foreign Bodies in the Auditory Canal." *Canadian Medical Review* 1, no. 5 (May 1895): 172–73.

Miller, Hanna. "Identity Takeout: How American Jews Made Chinese Food Their Ethnic Cuisine." *Journal of Popular Culture* 39, no. 3 (June 2006): 430–65.

Moerman, David E. *Native American Ethnobotany*. Portland, OR: Timber Press, 1998.

*Monetary Times, Trade Review and Insurance Chronicle*. "New Ontario" (September 7, 1900): 309. http://eco.canadiana.ca/view/oocihm.8_06569_949/19?r=0&s=3.

Moore, Geo. "Medicinal Properties of Some Herbs and Garden Vegetables." *Journal of Agriculture* 1, no. 10 (May 15, 1898): 145–60. http://eco.canadiana.ca/view/oocihm.8_06477_14/7?r=0&s=1.

Murray, Hugh. *An Encyclopaedia of Geography: Comprising a Complete Description of the Earth*. Vol. 2. Philadelphia: Carey, Lea and Blanchard, 1837.

Musselman, Lytton John. *Figs, Dates, Laurel and Myrrh: Plants of the Bible and Qu'ran*. Portland, OR: Timber Press, 2007.

Newman, Peter C. *The Canadian Establishment*. Toronto: McClelland & Stewart, 1999.

Oriental Express Central Asia. "Tash-Rabat Complex." http://www.kyrgyzstan.orexca.com/tash_rabat_kyrgyzstan.shtml.

Parker, James N., and Philip N. Parker. *Garlic: A Medical Dictionary, Bibliography, and Annotated Research Guide to Internet References*. San Diego, CA: ICON Health Publications, 2003.

Pizzorno, Joseph E. *Textbook of Natural Medicine*. London: Churchill Livingston, 2012.

Pospisil, Paul. "Growing Garlic from Bulbils." *Canadian Organic Grower* (Winter 2010): 12–15. https://www.cog.ca/uploads/TCOG%20 Articles/Growing%20garlic%20from%20bulbils.pdf.

PubMed Health. "How Does Our Sense of Taste Work?" U.S. National Library of Medicine, January 6, 2012. http://www.ncbi.nlm.nih.gov/ pubmedhealth/PMH0072592.

Renoux, Victoria. *For the Love of Garlic*. Garden City Park, NY: Square One Publishers, 2005.

Riendeau, Roger. *A Brief History of Canada*. New York: Infobase, 2007.

Rivlin, Richard S. "Historical Perspective on the Use of Garlic." *Journal of Nutrition* 131, no. 3 (March 1, 2001): 951S–54S.

Rombauer, Irma S., and Marion Rombauer. *Joy of Cooking*. Indianapolis, IN: Bobbs Merrill Company, 1964.

Rorer, Sarah Tyson. *Robin Hood Cookbook*. With historical notes by Elizabeth Driver. North Vancouver: Whitecap Books, 2003.

Sagard, Gabriel, and George M. Wrong. *Sagard's Long Journey to the Country of the Hurons*. Toronto: Champlain Society, 1939.

Schutyser, Tom. *Caravanserai: Traces, Places, Dialogue in the Middle East*. Milan: 5 Continents Editions, 2012.

Sellar, Gordon. *The Narrative of Gordon Sellar Who Emigrated to Canada in 1825*. Huntingdon, QC: Gleaner Book Room, 1915.

Short, Martin. *I Must Say: My Life as a Humble Comedy Legend*. London: Harper, 2014.

Sioui, Georges E. *Huron-Wendat: The Heritage of the Circle*. East Lansing: Michigan State University Press, 2000.

Small, Ernest. *North American Cornucopia*. Boca Raton, FL: CRC Press, 2013.

Smith, Andre. *Oxford Companion to American Food and Drink*. Oxford: Oxford University Press, 2009.

Smith, Annabelle. "Why the Tomato Was Feared in Europe for More than 200 Years," Smithsonian, June 18, 2013, Smithsonian.com.

Sturino, Frank, and John E. Zucchi. *Italians in Ontario*. Toronto: Multicultural History Society of Ontario, 1986.

Tamaki, K., T. Kamati and T. Yamazaki. "Studies on the Deodorization by Mushroom (*Agaricus bisporus*) Extract of Garlic Extract-Induced Oral Malodor." *Journal of Nutritional Science and Vitaminology* 53, no. 3 (June 2007): 277–86.

Tracey, Lindalee. *A Scattering of Seeds: The Creation of Canada*. Toronto: McArthur & Company, 1999.

Traill, Mrs. C.P. *The Female Emigrant's Guide, and Hints on Canadian Housekeeping*. Toronto: Maclear and Company, 1854.

Trustees' and Teachers Meeting, October 1, 1928. From archive of Secondary School No. 3, Neelon and Garson, Ontario. Copy of meeting note provided by Mary Stefura.

Tsurumi, Shunsuke. *An Intellectual History of Wartime Japan, 1931–1945*. New York: Routledge, 1986.

Washburn, Jennifer. "Science's Worst Enemy: Corporate Funding." *Discover Magazine* (October 11, 2007). http://discovermagazine.com/2007/oct/sciences-worst-enemy-private-funding.

Waugh, Daniel C. "The Mongols," Part II, "The World of Marco Polo and His Heirs." Wednesday University Lecture 4, 2002. University of Washington and Seattle Arts and Lectures.

Young, Kim. *Ethnobotany*. New York: Chelsea House, 2006.

Zohary, Daniel, et al. *Domestication of Plants in the Old World*. Oxford, UK: Oxford University Press, 2013.

# INDEX

# INDEX